Robin Thornbur
(260) 824-0203

More Splash Than Cash
Decorating Ideas

More Splash Than Cash™
Decorating Ideas

Over 1200 Tips, Tricks, Techniques,
and Ideas to Decorate Your Home

Donna Babylon

Windsor Oak
PUBLISHING

Library of Congress Cataloging-in-Publication Data

Babylon, Donna.
       More splash than cash decorating ideas: over 1200 tips, tricks, techniques, and ideas to decorate your home / Donna Babylon.
              p.   cm.
       Includes index
       ISBN: 0-9668227-0-6
       1. Interior decoration—Handbooks, manuals, etc. I. Title.
747—dc21   98—96971
                                                                        CIP

Cover, Interior Design, and Illustrations: Norm Myers
Illustrations by: Anne Davis Nunemacher
Cover Photography: T. R. Wailes
Editor: PeopleSpeak
Indexing: Directions Unlimited Desktop Services
Printed in the United States of America

10 9 8 7 6 5 4 3 2 1

Table of Contents

Table of Contents

Chapter 19: Helpful How-To's *(Continued)*

Introduction

Welcome to the world of decorating. You may feel that decorating your home is too challenging to attempt on your own, but with this book as your friendly guide, you'll see how simple it is to decorate your home—and how inexpensive it can be!

Packed with over 1200 tips, tricks, techniques, and ideas, this book invites you to decorate in a way that works for you whether you just want to spruce up your existing decor or you're starting from scratch in a home you've just moved into. You'll find yourself referring to this book often to find creative ways to decorate any room in your home. You'll be happy to note that these ideas are very easy to carry out (even if you think you have no talent) and inexpensive.

For example, do you hate your dark hand-me-down furniture? Bring it to life again with one of the many painting techniques explained in the furniture chapter.

Are you challenged by the concept of combining several different prints in one room? This book will give you the confidence to combine wallpaper, fabric, and paint to create a picture-perfect room.

Perhaps you moved into an apartment with limitations on what you can or can't do to the walls, ceilings, and floors. You'll find many ideas that are perfect for temporary dwellings. They create a homey feeling but can be picked up and transported to your next home without upsetting your present landlord.

In addition to these decorating tips and techniques, this book will teach you an important decorating philosophy: that you have permission to do whatever you want when you decorate. As you know, we live in a rule-dominated society. We stop at stop signs. We drive to the right of the yellow line. In decorating, however, there are no rules. And that's why we sometimes feel intimidated—we are looking for rules so we can proceed confidently. Instead of offering rules, I am giving you user-friendly guidelines. This way, if you decide to paint the four walls of a room in four different colors, you can do it and be confident the results will be outstanding.

This book also encourages you to be flexible, to have a sense of humor when decorating, and above all, to be fearless. It takes a lot of nerve to paint your bedroom purple. But if purple is your favorite color, then that's what color you should be using in your decorating.

How should you use this book? The layout is simple. Chapter 1 gives you some general tips and offers you a "game plan" to get you started. Then chapters 2–18 provide hundreds of ideas for all areas of your home. As you start to visualize many of the ideas, your plan for your room will come together. I intentionally did not include photographs in the book so that you can "see" the ideas your own way. You may not visualize exactly what I was thinking of when I wrote the tip, but you will see it applied in your room, in your home, and that will help you to make decisions that will work just for you.

Finally, chapter 19 gives you detailed instructions for selected projects mentioned in the book. There are projects for all skill levels. I hope you'll confidently try techniques that are new to you and create many beautiful projects. Along the way, you can refer to the glossary for definitions of decorating terms.

Decorating your home should be fun. With this book as your guide, you'll create a home that you love and a place you'll love to call home.

Acknowledgments

Many friends and professional associates shared their expertise during the writing of this book. All are experts in their own right, and I am deeply touched that they were so generous with their time and knowledge: Jeff and Beth Bill, Stephanie Caprarola, Rita Farrow, Jean Fidler, Jim Ford, Jon Garrett, Linda Griepentrog, Harriet Hargrave, Alice and Eric Haupt, Jeff Hughes, Maureen Klein, Linda Kreiling, Tom Mitchell, Andrea Niayz, Jane Sharp, Ginny Smith, Victoria Waller and Sheila Zent. I am forever grateful to Norm Myers whose enthusiasm and vision for this project is never-ending. And, without the guidance of my editor, Sharon Goldinger of PeopleSpeak, this book would not have the verbal sparkle and clarity it now has. Also the many professionals at The McCall Pattern Company who have been supportive of the overall concept of *More Splash Than Cash Decorating Ideas*.

1 Home Decorating Made Easy

Decorating doesn't have to cost a fortune. In fact, you'll enjoy your home even more knowing its million-dollar look cost next to nothing to create. With the tips in this book, you'll find it easy to create just the look you want no matter how small your budget is or how new to decorating you are.

Here's the first—and maybe the most important—tip you'll read here: always keep an open mind and a sense of humor when decorating your home. For example, you'll be surprised at what items you find in an alley the night before trash pickup. You may find it hard to adapt to this form of "shopping," but if you want to be a budget-minded decorator, you can't be a snob.

HOW DO I BEGIN?

Cost-Effective Decorating Strategies

Before you get started, consider these approaches to achieve the look you're after. Compare these ideas when making choices.

❀ Paint spreads more style for less money than any other decorating basic. My friend Ginny once told me, "When in doubt—paint it!" This is great advice.

❀ When selecting items for your home, choose pieces of furniture, artwork, lamps, and so on, that you like. Don't worry if everything doesn't match. You can use paint and fabric to achieve a harmonious, "pulled-together" look.

1 – Home Decorating Made Easy

☀ Stroll through a fine furniture store for ideas and inspiration. Many times, these stores arrange furniture in attractive settings and you'll get great ideas for fabric and paint combinations.

☀ Evaluate your budget and allow more money for some areas of a room than others. For example, invest in the best quality slipcovers and curtains that you can afford. Then head to your favorite discount stores for accessory items such as pillows, lamps, throw rugs, and framed pictures.

☀ One of my favorite "shopping" places is my mom's house. I go through the basement, the attic, the garage to

Bringing a Room to Life

Sometimes, it's the simple things that can take a room from being so-so to becoming sensational. Consider these suggestions for creating an interesting room.

- Determine what shapes dominate the room you are decorating. Look at the shapes of your sofa, television, tables, bed, dresser, and so on. If the majority of the lines are squares or rectangles, add some interesting accessories that are circular in shape.

see what has been disposed of. I refer to my dining room furniture pieces as "early basement." (You might want to "shop" at your aunt's and grandmother's houses, too!)

☀ "One man's trash is another man's treasure" couldn't be more true for the budget-minded decorator. Look for bargains everywhere! Investigate discount furniture stores, secondhand stores, antique malls, flea markets, swap meets, estate auctions, and garage sales. Also try storage companies. They often sell—at very low cost—items that have been left unclaimed in their facilities.

- Do you have either (1) a lot of fabric-covered items in the room or (2) a lot of matching wood surfaces? This sameness can be boring to the eye. An easy solution is to introduce other surfaces or textures such as smooth glass, shiny metallics, or even baskets and rugs. Consider using opposite textures within the same room: rough and smooth, dark and light, shiny and dull.

- Arrange the accessories in the room so they are at different eye levels. For example, use two different-sized table lamps in the same room or group together some accessories that are of different heights on a shelf, mantel, or side table.

- Make sure to include area rugs that are in proportion to your furnishings. They will tie the room together.

- Include plenty of green plants in your decorating scheme for texture and a touch of nature. Make the plants part of the furniture grouping— don't place them off on their own.

- To include your artwork in the decorating scheme, connect it to other furnishings by hanging it 6 to 9 inches above the furniture, or group several wall items together.

1 – Home Decorating Made Easy

※ Have a plan before you go shopping so you are on the lookout for the pieces that you need. However, if you find a real treasure that is not on your list, but you can visualize its potential in your home, go ahead and buy it.

※ Be alert when driving along the road. Sometimes objects are simply discarded and left along the roadside waiting for your creative touch. You may have heard about people who found the perfect sofa for their home along an old country road. This, too, could happen to you!

※ Don't ignore slightly flawed antiques. Evidence of a little wear and tear adds character and charm to furniture and accessories. Besides, they are usually a lot less expensive than antiques in mint condition.

※ Look for well-built furniture pieces. If repairs are needed, make sure you can do them inexpensively and that you can hide the repair with paint and/or fabric.

※ Window treatments don't have to be lavish or conform to some traditional style. Not only fabrics of all kinds, but wood and even houseplants can be placed in front of a window to act as creative, yet inexpensive, window dressings. Imagine fence posts, hats, or kitchen utensils hanging over your windows!

WHERE CAN I FIND GREAT BARGAINS?

※ Throw rugs are less expensive and more versatile than wall-to-wall carpeting, and they can be quickly changed and used seasonally.

※ Mismatched flatware is much more interesting (and inexpensive) than a matched set.

※ Trust your instincts when making purchasing decisions. Avoid the pressure to buy if you feel the item is over-priced. Wait for sales.

※ Remember that baskets are inexpensive, versatile, and essential decorating tools. Fill them with flowers, magazines, potpourri, fireplace logs, and even guest towels.

☀ Decorate from the heart. You are the one who has to live with them, so buy items you love.

☀ Don't be afraid to make mistakes. More than likely, what you think is a mistake will not be noticed by others who enter your home.

☀ Don't play it safe. If you do, you'll never do what you really want to.

WHERE DO I GET DECORATING IDEAS TO USE IN MY HOME?

First-Time Decorating

Moving into a first home is one occasion when nearly everyone needs low-cost decorating ideas like the ones in this book. But just because you're short of cash doesn't mean you have to be short on style.

Now that you are on your own, you want to make a personal style statement, but you may not know where or how to start. You probably feel torn between wanting to make your own decisions and needing to rely on the advice of others who have some decorating experience. Follow these suggestions to ensure that your first-time decorating efforts will be a success.

☀ If you are having a hard time selecting a color scheme, turn to your closet. What colors do you like to wear? If you like wearing certain colors, you will certainly enjoy living with those same colors.

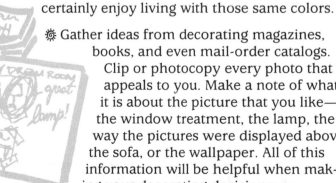

☀ Gather ideas from decorating magazines, books, and even mail-order catalogs. Clip or photocopy every photo that appeals to you. Make a note of what it is about the picture that you like— the window treatment, the lamp, the way the pictures were displayed above the sofa, or the wallpaper. All of this information will be helpful when making your decorating decisions.

☀ Organize your selections in a large file with subcategories such as painting techniques, furniture arrangements, and faux finishing techniques. Carefully file your ideas in the appropriate places.

1 – Home Decorating Made Easy

☼ Wait a few days before going through your files. Sit down with a friend or a roommate to review your ideas. Your notes will help you to explain what originally caught your eye in the photographs. Discard any clippings that no longer appeal to you.

☼ While you are going over the photos, start a new list that summarizes what you like. Be specific when making your list and use as many descriptive words as possible: the apple green paint on the walls, the ivy trellis placed behind the bed, the stenciled floral border around the doorway, the flower arrangements, or the green, white, and lilac rug.

☼ Analyze what your lists are telling you. Have you mentioned *floral* wallpaper several times? Has a particular *color* been mentioned over and over? How about a *stenciled* floor? If you listed something over and over, that is a good starting point for your decorating efforts.

☼ Save the photos and refer back to them often as you build toward your goal of decorating your first home.

☼ Buy one piece of furniture that you can't live without and make this piece the focal point of the room.

☼ Turn furniture shopping into an adventure. Be a regular at flea markets and shop at yard sales religiously (go first thing in the morning for the best selection). Make friends at your local second-hand store to find out when new merchandise arrives. Be there when they take the new stuff off the truck!

☼ Even though there are a variety of fabric prints and patterns available, you'll probably be drawn to one or two particular styles. If you fall in love with a fabric, rest assured that you will not tire of it easily.

☼ Refer to this book often for ideas to use throughout the house.

Redecorate with What You Have

Bored with your decor but not in a position to do a complete overhaul? Don't despair! Sometimes just changing one or two features in the room will give it the boost it needs. The secret is to find items you already have in your house that can be used in another room and possibly in a different way. If you use your imagination and look carefully around your home, you'll find plenty of interesting items to adapt to new uses. Use the following ideas to get your own creative juices flowing.

☀ Display your collection of antique plates on the wall in your bathroom or bedroom—not in the dining room.

☀ Search through your drawers and closets. Hang items with interesting shapes on the wall—kitchen utensils, baskets, hats, trays, or memorabilia.

☀ Gather together old photographs of your family or the area where you live, frame them, and then display them as a grouping in any room of your home.

☀ Tack a piece of particularly pretty fringe or cording from a fabric store or secondhand shop to the wall over a painting or around a window. Use small finishing nails to attach the fringe to the wall.

☀ Move some furniture pieces to new positions. For example, move a desk that has been against the wall so it sits diagonally in a corner.

☀ Do you have any pieces of wallpaper left over from when you papered your bedroom, kitchen, or bath? Turn them into colorful accent pieces by covering a plain wastebasket, a lampshade, and desk accessories.

☀ Interchange your lamps from your living room and your bedroom. If the bases of the lamps don't fit in with their new positions, cut a large circle of fabric, center the lamp in the middle of it, and gather the fabric at the neck of the lamp for a completely new look. Secure the gathers in place with a piece of decorative cording. Tuck under any raw edges for a nice finish.

☀ Arrange assorted cookie cutters on an empty wall in the kitchen area.

☀ Use an old trunk from the attic or even a wooden storage chest as a coffee table.

☀ Move your loveseat from the living room to the dining room and use it to replace a few of the dining room chairs.

☀ Use vases in all shapes, sizes, and textures to hold candles, potpourri, and colored glass chips.

☀ Create an additional conversation area in any room with two armchairs and an accent table that were found in another room.

☀ Move your wall decorations from the hallway into the living room.

☀ Introduce the unexpected into the bathroom. Bring in a dining room chair to hold towels or use a chest of drawers or an armoire for a decorative storage spot.

☀ For even more ideas, refer to "Something from Nothing," page 59 in the Furniture chapter.

Do-It-Yourself Advice

Do-it-yourself projects are very appealing because we would like to take credit when someone admires our home. But don't become disillusioned over the size of the job(s) at hand. Consider these helpful pointers.

I'VE ALWAYS ADMIRED PEOPLE WHO HAVE DECORATED THEIR HOMES BY THEMSELVES. HOW CAN I DO IT, TOO?

☀ Don't underestimate the amount of time it will take to do a project. Be sure to allow the time it will take to gather all of the necessary supplies and equipment. Also consider your skill level. If you are new to a type of project— putting up wallpaper, for example—it will take longer.

☀ If you can, solicit a partner to work with and use each other's abilities to the best advantage when planning a project.

☀ Before diving into a project, brainstorm the process first. By taking this step, you'll be able to anticipate potential problems and have ready solutions.

☀ Know what you want before you begin. This step can be as simple as writing down a list of decorating ideas you want incorporated into your room. Refer to your file of photos from magazines of accessories or techniques you like.

☀ After you have developed a decorating plan, sleep on it. If you're patient, you'll find that your ideas just keep getting better and better.

☀ If you are redecorating, make your house as comfortable as possible during this process. Make it a rule to straighten up at the end of each workday. You'll appreciate the neater environment.

☀ Work on one room at a time. You'll be more focused and more inclined to continue your decorating endeavors if you can see each room completed before you go on to the next one.

Tool Time

The first rule of do-it-yourselfers should be to use proper tools. Don't try to use makeshift tools to accomplish a task. Keep all of your small tools together in a portable heavy-duty tackle or toolbox so everything you need will be within reach. Here is a list of the basic tools you'll need for decorating projects.

Painting: Drop cloths, brushes, a roller and tray, tack cloth or a vacuum cleaner, a pail, sponges, drying cloths, mineral spirits or cleaning solvent, masking tape, Spackle, putty knife, sandpaper, and a stepladder.

Wallpapering: Scissors, a wallpaper brush for smoothing out the paper, sponges, a utility knife, a straight edge, a stepladder, a seam roller, a plumb line, chalk, and a water tray.

Woodworking and Carpentry: A drill and bits, screwdrivers (Phillips and standard), a saw (jigsaw, miter saw, or circular saw, depending on the project), a retractable metal tape measure, a level, a utility knife, nails of various sizes, an assortment of wood and drywall screws, nuts, bolts and washers, a staple gun, a hammer, wall anchors, pliers (standard and needle-nose), vise grips, an adjustable wrench, C-clamps, wood glue, sandpaper and an electric or hand sander, a miter box, a nail set, a stud finder, T-square or L-square, and protective goggles.

Sewing: A sewing machine with zigzag stitch capabilities, straight pins, machine needles in various sizes for different types of fabric, handsewing needles, a tape measure, fabric scissors, a hem gauge, a seam ripper, a T-square or L-square, a right angle triangle, a yardstick, tailor's chalk or a fabric marking pen, an iron and a large, flat ironing surface, a press cloth, and seam sealant.

2 Color Your World

You really can't decorate without color. Because color affects the mood of the room directly and indirectly, the choice of color in a room is crucial. A whole room changes instantly with creative use of color.

Colorful Thoughts

We see so many colors all around us but when it comes to selecting and committing to colors to live with, color can become a problem. How do you approach adding color to your world? Here are some ideas to help you choose the right colors for you.

☀ How do you decide on a color theme? You might use the colors in a fabric you fall in love with, a painting, or even a piece of wallpaper. You might also want to look in your closet again at the colors you like to wear.

☀ To develop a personal color sense, look through magazines and clip photos of what catches your eye. The clippings may seem unrelated at first but you'll gradually see a pattern develop in your preferences.

☀ Before you start to redo a room, ask for input from the people who live with you. They'll be living there, too.

☀ Begin with existing furnishings to build a color scheme.

☀ When painting your room a new color, give yourself time

to adjust to a drastic change. Remember, it's only paint and can be changed quickly.

☀ You don't have to select a drab color like white, off-white, beige, or cream to be practical. Bright colors do not show dirt any more than their paler counterparts.

☀ Limit the number of principal colors that are used in one room to three or four. Repeat each color several times throughout the room to achieve a uniform look.

Color Effects

Have you ever purchased an outfit in the store only to find out at home that the colors don't match as well as you thought? Different lighting affects how we see color. Keep this important consideration in mind when selecting color for your world.

☀ Consider the location and setting of your home when selecting your color scheme. For example, a country setting lends itself well to neutral colors, crisp blues and whites, and deep greens.

☀ Always check colors in both artificial and natural light before making a definite decision.

☀ Color creates a mood. Whether you want the room to be subdued and quiet or lively and full of energy will affect your color choice.

☀ Textures affect colors. For example, a rough or shiny surface will give the same hue a different look. Shiny finishes (glossy enamels, polished metals, and mirrors) visually enhance the size of the room; plush or matte textures makes a room seem cozy. Translucent lace or sheers are less imposing visually than heavy drapes.

☀ East-facing windows get strong morning light, but during the rest of the day the light is not overpowering. That means the color you select will be most intense in the early morning but softer the rest of the day. Keep this fact in mind when selecting colors for your bedroom as the highest-impact color will be what you see first when waking in the morning.

WHY DO COLORS ALWAYS SEEM DIFFERENT IN MY HOUSE THAN IN THE STORE?

☀ Rooms with a south or west orientation receive the hottest light during the day. This means the color in these rooms will have extra punch. You may need to select paint a shade or two lighter to get the color you want.

☀ A room with a northern exposure won't get much influence from Mother Nature. It's the coolest room in the house and has the most consistent natural lighting.

☀ Color can camouflage the height, width, and length of a room. To make a room seem taller, use white on the ceiling. To make a high ceiling seem lower, use a dark color on it. To make a long room look shorter, paint the walls on the short sides of the room a darker color than the remaining two.

An Eye for Color

It's a proven fact that colors affect our moods, eating habits, purchasing habits, and even our ability to learn. Creative use of color will certainly do wonders for every room in your home. Remember these general principals about what color does to a room as you choose the colors you'll live with.

☀ Warm colors such as red and yellow will warm up a room; cool colors such as blue and green will cool it down. Select cool colors for a room that receives lots of sunlight and warm colors for a shady room.

☀ Cool colors are fresh and soothing. Certain shades of purple, blue, and green can visually create an illusion of space in otherwise tight quarters. Rich, warm colors such as red, yellow, and brown create a cozy environment in a large room.

☀ A neutral color scheme incorporating interesting textures—stucco walls, velvet throw pillows, and sisal rugs—will add spatial interest and good visual balance to any room.

☀ Bold colors are not overwhelming in a room if they're used in small amounts. Keep in mind that color is intensified when it is used in large quantities. The color that's just right in an accent pillow may overwhelm the room if it is used on large areas such as the walls.

2 – Color Your World

❋ Colors unify patterns. When putting several patterned fabrics together in one room, select prints that contain the same colors. In this way you can use plaids, stripes, and florals together without creating visual chaos.

❋ Test your color choice first. Buy a small amount of paint and paint several very large pieces of white cardboard the color you have selected for the walls. Hang them around the room so you can observe the color and how it looks throughout the day. Live with the boards for a while to see if you need to make any adjustments.

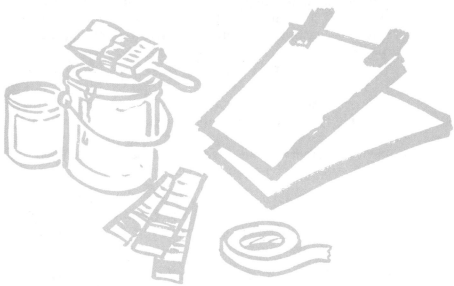

Mad about Hue

Having fun with color is one of the most exciting aspects of home decorating. A dash of color here and a splash of color there add to the personality of the room.

❋ Colored light bulbs add a subtle layer of color. Pink ones soften a space (and are more flattering to skin tones) while pale yellow bulbs give an antique glow.

❋ Use fresh fruit or a bouquet of flowers to add color to a room.

❋ Flowering plants available in rich pinks, reds, and purples are an inexpensive, yet very effective, way to add color to a room.

※ Stained glass placed in front of a window (even small "sun catchers") will add color and sparkle to any room when the sunlight shines through it.

I'VE ALWAYS HAD WHITE WALLS BUT NOW I'M BORED WITH THEM. HOW CAN I ADD SOMETHING MORE EXCITING?

※ Add exciting splashes of primary colors to an otherwise dull, white room. High-gloss paint will add more drama than flat paint.

※ When planning a color scheme for a new baby's room, consider using neutral colors for the walls and flooring. The color scheme will develop as fabric accessories such as a dust ruffle or a valance are added to the room.

※ Are you still apprehensive about painting a room a color other than white or off-white? Try the color for a while in smaller quantities (for example, by adding a few throw pillows) to see how you like it.

※ When selecting colors for adjoining rooms, blend colors from one area to another to create color unity. For example, if your living room is yellow with blue accents and the adjoining dining room is blue, add some yellow accents to the dining room so the colors flow together.

※ The oldest of bathrooms will look years younger when everything is painted white. Add color with posters, towels, and baskets full of colorful and fragrant soaps.

※ Robust colors usually appeal to men. Avoid floral or pastel hues when decorating a room for a man. Try hunter green and tan, burgundy and navy, or autumn tones such as gold, terra cotta, and brown.

※ Special interests or hobbies may be the inspiration for a color scheme or decorating theme.

※ Emphasize architectural details such as molding and trim by painting them a darker or lighter shade than the walls.

※ Select a ceiling color that will enhance the wall color. For example, paint your dining room a wonderful shade of burgundy, and the ceiling an opulent gold.

In Living Color

There are no right or wrong color choices when decorating the different rooms in your home. However, since color does affect the mood of its occupants, consider what a room is used for when you choose a color to paint the walls. Here are some ideas to get you started.

Living Room

Any warm color is a good choice for this room. Warm colors include reds, yellows, and oranges and all shades and hues of these color families. Shades of pink and peach encourage people to be more social.

Dining Room

Dark red is the optimal choice for a dining area, especially if you entertain a lot, because it encourages conversation and appetite. Ruby red is a particularly good color as it awakens the mind and encourages people to talk openly. Avoid white, which doesn't create an intimate feeling.

Den/Study/Home Office

Green is the color of choice for this area of the house because it encourages concentration. Brown is associated with warmth and comfort and is also a good choice.

Kitchen

Red may be too aggressive a color for a kitchen as it stimulates the appetite. Green would be a better selection because it implies natural food and health. Bright yellow is associated with lemon freshness and cheerfulness, but it may be a little too stimulating for a kitchen environment because it makes you want to eat quickly.

Bedroom

To evoke a peaceful feeling in the bedroom, select a shade of green, the color associated with comfort, quietness, and relaxation. Blues and purples are also calming—and sophisticated. Pinks and peaches are warm and inviting.

Bathroom

Pink and peach colors make people look as if they have a natural, healthy glow, but yellow produces just the opposite effect. Pink and peach also help you release tension and heighten your spirits if you are depressed. Blue creates a meditative atmosphere. White gives the impression that the room is clean and sterile. If you need to have some help waking up in the morning, select a bright red or green for your bathroom.

3 Ceilings and Walls

*T*hink of the ceilings and walls of your home as blank canvases just waiting for your creative touch. Creative opportunities abound for these large surfaces.

Heads Up!

Take decorating to new heights by treating the ceiling as one of the walls in a room. It can match or contrast with the other walls. Adding one of these lofty ideas is not complicated, and your effort will be repaid with a great-looking room.

❂ Make a low ceiling appear higher by painting it a color lighter than the walls. Another way to create the illusion of height is to install crown molding directly on the ceiling instead of on the wall. The eye will see the molding as part of the wall, and the ceiling will seem higher.

❂ To make a high ceiling seem lower, place the crown molding slightly below the ceiling line (where the wall and ceiling meet), and then paint the wall above the molding in the same color as the ceiling.

❂ Another way to make a high ceiling appear lower is to cover the walls with a light-colored wallpaper to contrast with the dark-colored ceiling.

❂ Paint the ceiling to coordinate with your wallpaper. Select a paint color that will blend with and not detract from your selected wallpaper.

3 – Ceilings and Walls

❋ You can even use wallpaper on the ceiling. A word of caution: Select a soothing design for a bedroom ceiling as you'll be looking at it a lot when you're lying in bed.

❋ Instead of wallpapering the entire ceiling, stencil a design in the corners.

❋ Marbleize, paint, or stamp ceiling panels (used for a dropped ceiling) before installing.

❋ Paint stars or clouds on the ceiling in a child's room to create a fantasy outdoor canopy.

❋ Extend fabric panels across the ceiling. Stitch rod pockets in both ends of the fabric panel and install it on ceiling-mounted curtain rods. If your ceiling is extra-wide, you may need additional supports (available where drapery hardware is sold) spaced at equal distances.

❋ Traditional moldings add elegance and sophistication to a room. Plastic or polyurethane foam varieties are readily available in do-it-yourself stores. These products are very easy to work with and many come with premitered (precut) corners and predrilled nail holes. As an added bonus, they are primed and ready for paint.

❋ Create a ceiling border with two parallel lines of molding that go around the perimeter of the room and are spaced 4 to 6 inches apart. Between the molding strips, paint the ceiling a darker color and add a wallpaper border or interesting medallions. Consider painting the main portion of the ceiling a medium color, the molding a crisp white, and the space between the molding strips a medium-to-dark color.

❋ If the walls throughout your house are monochromatic, create a new color scheme by painting the ceilings of each room a different color.

❋ You can use embossed wallpapers to simulate the look of an old-fashioned tin ceiling. Cover the entire ceiling with this type of paper and extend it a little way down each wall to create the illusion of a high ceiling. Hang decorative crown molding to cover the paper's bottom edge. Finally, paint the wallpaper with semi-gloss paint.

☀ Paint the blades of a ceiling fan in a color that coordinates with the rest of the room, especially the ceiling treatment. If the ceiling is faux finished (such as ragging), consider using the same technique on the ceiling fan blades. Other blade-decorating options include wallpaper or stencils.

Up Against a Wall

Paint and wallpaper are the first kinds of wall treatments that come to mind, and they'll be covered in detail in this chapter. But for some different and often smaller projects for your walls, try these.

☀ Create a shadowed image on your wall by lighting a large house plant or tree from below. The shadows of the leaves that this uplighting produces will be interesting to the eye.

☀ A quick fix for a problem wall is to add texture. This can be easily done with drywall joint compound. Working in a 4-foot-square area, apply a layer of compound (about 1/8 to 1/4 inch thick). Then drag a 6-inch drywall knife down the wall to create a background texture. Excess compound will accumulate on the knife during this process. Simply reapply the compound on the knife as if you were icing a cake. Once the area is covered, add surface texture with a plastic kitchen scrubber (steel wool rusts) by randomly patting it against the wall. Or use a special stucco brush, sponge, or comb. Allow the wall to dry completely (at least 24 hours) before painting it. Always prime the surface before you paint (if you don't, the compound will soak up the paint). For an even coat of paint on rough surfaces, use a roller brush with a 1-inch nap.

☀ Instead of actually applying a textured surface to the wall, use a textured wallpaper or border that can be painted any color. This is a perfect solution to cover dark paneling or problem walls.

3 – Ceilings and Walls

☀ If you have ceramic-tiled walls in the bathroom and shower, consider replacing a row or two with a different color. Another option would be to intersperse colored tile throughout the room.

☀ Create a miniature mural on one wall with a variety of tiles and tile pieces. Consider using a popular quilt design from a quilt book and duplicate the look with mix-and-match tiles. Vary the color and textures if possible.

☀ A collection of old theater marquee letters, old printing blocks, or any other three-dimensional letters grouped together on a wall, on a shelf, or over a mantel can offer greetings or other messages to your houseguests.

☀ If you have a room without a view, create one. Paint or stencil a favorite outdoor scene on canvas, then arrange wide wooden molding strips around the perimeter of the canvas to create a "window" frame.

☀ Architectural interest can be easily added to a room by installing decorative molding to plain walls. You can create vertical floor-to-ceiling panels with lengths of molding arranged to make rectangles. Geometric patterns are another creative molding option. Consider making squares or diamonds of molding at chair-rail height. Fill the area within the framed shapes with wallpaper, contrasting paint, or even a picture or a mirror.

☀ Collect several old pieces of slate or chalkboards. Have the younger members of your family apply their artistic touches to the surface with chalk. Display the "art gallery" on a wall. These chalkboards would be perfect wall decor for a kitchen, hallway, or foyer.

☀ Recreate a motif found in your wallpaper, fabric, or china pattern in stencil form and stencil these designs around the perimeter of the room. (See page 193 for complete instructions on this technique.)

☼ A relatively simple way to dress up walls is to add wainscoting (wood paneling that reaches part way up the walls). It's easy to install and is the perfect wall treatment for any room in the house. Wainscot kits are available from hardware stores. This treatment is a good way to camouflage imperfect walls.

☼ Traditionally, wainscoting is installed 30 to 32 inches up from the floor. Paint the wainscoting one color and the wall another, or add wallpaper to the wall above the wainscoting.

☼ If you plan to use sheet paneling as your wainscoting, cut one 48 by 96 inch board crosswise into thirds (each 32 inches high) for maximum use of a panel sheet.

☼ Add moldings to wainscoting for a traditional look. Select from a variety of top and bottom moldings that come in a variety of widths and styles. Why not paint the molding in a contrasting color for additional impact?

☼ For uneven or damaged walls, apply paneling to camouflage all of the defects. You can find paneling that mimics the look of wallpaper, ceramic tiles, stone, or woodgrains.

Molding: What Goes Where

Here are some common types of molding and their usual locations on the wall.

- Chair rails are placed 30 to 36 inches above the floor and act as bumpers so that chair backs don't mark the walls.

- Crown molding is usually placed at the ceiling line or "crown" of the room directly on the wall.

- Plate-rail molding is placed 10 to 12 inches down from the ceiling line on the wall. It has a ledge used to display plates or pictures along the wall.

- Single shelves are placed around the perimeter of the room about 2 feet from the ceiling.

3 – Ceilings and Walls

☀ Write personal messages around the room on the walls. Refer to books of quotations for inspiration. Or use an original poem. Write your words on a white sheet of paper and project them on the wall with an overhead projector (maybe you can borrow one from your local school). Then simply trace over the projected words with your permanent marker.

☀ For a child's room, write freehand the words to a favorite nursery rhyme or bedtime story on the wall. Use an air-erasable marker to set up guidelines for the lettering.

☀ Provide your guests with different-colored permanent markers and have them write messages, sayings, or whatever crosses their minds on your bathroom wall. This is a colorful and inexpensive alternative to wall-paper—and a real attention getter!

☀ Removable wall decals are the perfect choice when decorating a nursery because they allow you to redeco-rate easily as the child gets older.

☀ Paint an accent wall a different color than the others. The accent can be dramatic (for example, three light walls with one dark green wall for the accent) or subtle (white walls with a beige accent). Select a wall where furniture pieces will be placed for the accent wall. For example, paint the wall behind a bed the accent color.

☀ Here's an idea for the walls of a child's room—but it's not for the fainthearted. Fill up squirt guns with bright colors of latex wall paints that have been thinned with water. Have one or more budding painters, under supervision, of course, decorate the walls with squirts of color. Note: If the paint does not come out of the squirt gun, even after thinning, make the hole slightly larger.

Fireside Chat

Unquestionably, fireplaces add visual and actual warmth to a room. Not all of us are fortunate enough to have a built-in fireplace, but we can create an illusion of one with a little ingenuity.

☼ Individual molding pieces can create this illusion. To add depth to this accent, paint the wall inside the fireplace "opening" a dark color.

☼ Another imaginary fireplace can be created with a drawing of a fireplace from a period architectural sketchbook. A photo copying service can enlarge the picture to life size. You can also use an overhead projector. Transfer the design to the wall and paint it.

Here are some ideas for those lucky enough to have a real fireplace.

☼ Paint the mantel and trim a warm, rich color that complements the color scheme already in the room.

☼ During the months when it is not working, fill the fireplace with fresh or silk flowers or even a collection of candles and candlesticks.

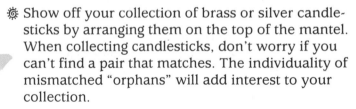

☼ Show off your collection of brass or silver candlesticks by arranging them on the top of the mantel. When collecting candlesticks, don't worry if you can't find a pair that matches. The individuality of mismatched "orphans" will add interest to your collection.

☼ Accent your mantel arrangement by placing items in front of a shiny tray or mirror that stands on its edge and reflects your collection.

☼ Display themed accessories such as clocks of all shapes and sizes as a collection on a mantel.

☼ Cover the opening of a fireplace with a colorful fireplace screen. Make your own screen from shelving and folding screen hinges. Add a fabric slipcover to the vertical panels for a softer look and feel. The slipcover panels can be changed seasonally. (See page 189 for complete instructions for this project.)

Mirror Images

"Mirror, mirror" is on the wall and anywhere else you can think of! This essential decorating accessory creates a multitude of looks and images.

☀ Embellish a plain mirror by adding picture-frame molding to the outside edges. Practice cutting and joining the molding at a 45 degree angle for mitered corners. Use a miter box lined with sandpaper to keep the molding from slipping while you cut. Paint the molding before affixing it to the mirror. Once the paint is dry, glue the frame to the mirror with an epoxy glue that works with metal and wood. You may need to fill in gaps with wood putty; touch up the patches with paint if needed.

☀ For the best reflection, position a mirror opposite a light source.

☀ Hang a collection of small antique mirrors together to create an illusion of extra space.

☀ Install a mirror between a pair of windows to give the illusion of one large window.

☀ Use a convex mirror (the kind they use in stores to spot shoplifters) as an amusing wallhanging.

☀ Select a space on the wall for a mirror that will provide an interesting reflection. For example, hang a mirror opposite a door or window.

☀ Create an Art Deco effect by arranging mirror squares diagonally on an otherwise bare wall. For added impact, paint the wall a dark color so the mirrors will truly sparkle.

☀ Line up a series of rectangular mirrors along one wall. These mirrors are readily available in discount stores. Paint the frames to coordinate with your room.

☀ In the bathroom, hang a mirror over the sink suspended by a wire camouflaged with a beautiful ribbon and attached to a ceiling hook. Make sure the ceiling hook is installed in a stud so it will support a heavy object such as a mirror.

❀ Install a floor-length mirror in your foyer. Frame the mirror with decorative molding and add louvered doors on each side. The visual effect is a pleasing sense of spaciousness.

Wallpaper Wonders

Nothing sets a mood faster than wallpaper. Available in virtually any print, theme, or color scheme imaginable, this addition to your room will produce wonderful results!

WHAT SHOULD I CONSIDER WHEN SELECTING WALLPAPER?

❀ To make wallpaper work best for you, select a paper in a bright color if your room has a northern exposure and in a duller color if your room has a southern exposure. If your walls are badly damaged, select a dark paper or one with a very busy pattern to conceal defects.

❀ If selecting wallpaper for the first time, keep in mind that vinyl and vinyl-coated wallcoverings are the easiest to hang and can be pulled off and rehung if you make a mistake.

❀ After you have fallen in love with a wallpaper pattern, take the largest available sample home with you and live with it for a while before you commit to the pattern permanently.

❀ For maximum impact, select large-scale patterns, dense patterns, and dark colors.

❀ When selecting wallpaper or borders for your bathroom, don't limit yourself to the sample books that focus on bathrooms.

❀ Don't be afraid to use two different wallpapers in one room. Select a strong print for one wall and a more subtle, yet coordinating, print for the others.

❀ If you feel even more adventurous, use three wallpaper prints in one room. Follow this basic formula for success with three patterns: select a large-scale print, a medium geometric print (this could be a border), and a small print. Blend the colors and prints, rather than matching. Try to select the wallpapers from the same manufacturer so the colors match exactly.

❀ Combine wallpaper and faux-finishes on the same wall. For example, duplicate a full-sized quilt by using wallpaper cutouts (shaped like a star, a square, a diamond, and so on) to make patterned quilt blocks. Alternate with plain blocks made using a faux finish painting technique such as rag rolling or sponging.

❀ Take advantage of wallpaper closeouts. However, you may not find enough of one wallpaper design to complete your project. Consider adding a coordinating wallpaper or two and install them side by side on the walls.

❀ Always start with a clean surface before hanging wallpaper. Even a fine layer of dust can interfere with the adhesive. Vacuum or dust the walls before starting.

❀ Remove the switch plates and outlet covers before wallpapering. When the wallpaper is dry, cut away the excess paper from the openings with a utility knife and then replace the fittings over the switches and outlets.

Head for the Borders

If wallpapering a whole room is beyond your budget, design the room around one of the wonderful decorative wall borders that are available. A border of any kind adds instant coziness to any room in a home. As with all decorating endeavors, there are no rules when using borders.

❀ Use a border to camouflage a room's size. Place the border at the top of the wall to make a ceiling seem higher. Place the border at picture or chair-rail level to make the ceiling appear lower.

❀ In the kitchen, place a narrow border between the space under the cabinets and the top of the back splash.

❀ Create a "headboard" behind a bed with a border; use matching fabric or sheets in the room for a complete setting. Add narrow molding strips along the top and bottom edges of the border for an accent.

❀ Place a border print on the back panel of a bookshelf for added color in a room.

❀ Follow the natural lines of a stairway with a border to make a decorating statement.

❀ Show off any architectural features such as a well-shaped doorway or an interesting ceiling—one that slopes, for example—by outlining the area with a border.

❀ Fill in an otherwise empty corner by placing border strips vertically on each adjoining wall with the inside edges of the border touching.

❀ Create a frame with a border to highlight your favorite piece of art or a collection of photographs.

❀ Use a border to frame a window, chair rail, baseboard, or crown molding.

❀ To create a sense of formality in your dining room, frame the ceiling perimeter, then add a border around the chandelier in the shape of an octagon, square, or diamond.

❀ Add a border inside the arch of a doorway between two rooms.

❀ Place a border between two rows of decorative molding that are painted a coordinating color. This combination could be used as a chair rail or as visual interest on the wall around the perimeter of the room against the ceiling.

❀ Use a border to mat a piece of artwork or favorite photograph.

❀ Add a border to the risers of a staircase.

❀ Unify all the elements of a room by running a continuous border around all of its architectural and decorative components.

❀ Use two coordinating borders for maximum impact. Place one at the top of the wall and another at chair-rail height.

❀ Add a border strip to the bottom edge of a roller shade to coordinate with the border in the rest of the room.

❀ Use a border to simulate raised panels on a door; frame the border with decorative molding.

3 – Ceilings and Walls

❋ Use leftover pieces of a border to cover accessories such as an accordion file, a wastebasket, a desk set, a light-switch cover, hatboxes, picture frames, canisters, and a lampshade. (See the following tip.)

❋ Use a wide paper border to make a lampshade, a welcome accessory for any room in your home. Simply measure the bottom circumference of a lampshade frame and multiply by 2 for the length of border needed. (The selected border needs to be slightly wider than the shade's height.) Accordion pleat the border into folds about 1 inch deep. With a hole punch, punch a hole around the top edge in the middle of each pleat. Run a narrow ribbon through the holes, place the folded border over the lampshade frame, and tighten the ribbon to fit the top edge of the frame. Tie the ribbon into a bow to secure the lampshade.

Border Patrol

When you think of borders, you might automatically think of wallpaper borders. The selection of wallpaper borders is indeed immense, but you can create your own borders, too, with a little ingenuity.

❋ Show off your favorite vacation photos by making color copies of same-size photos, laminating them, and arranging them side by side around the perimeter of the room. Add thin molding strips to the top and bottom edges of the photos to frame the images if desired.

❋ Create a decorative border from 1/2-inch plywood and small ceramic tiles. Plan the tile design on graph paper (refer to quilt blocks for inspiration) before cutting the plywood into strips wide enough to accommodate the tile design and as long as the room. Install the plywood strips where you want the borders around the perimeter of the room (use screws placed 6 inches apart). Glue the tiles directly to the wood in a pleasing pattern. Apply grout over the tiles, working it into the spaces between them. Allow the grout to dry before sponging off the excess. For a professional finishing touch, install a thin molding strip (that has already been painted or stained) along the top and bottom edges of this newly created border.

How to Hang a Wall Border

Many borders come prepasted to make installation a breeze. Other types available are those that are repositionable and those that require wallpaper paste. For all types of wall border, simply measure off the amount you need (equal to the measurement from corner to corner plus a few inches to wrap into corners). Activate prepasted adhesive or apply adhesive if necessary. Fold and "book" the border (fold strip over on itself with pasted sides touching) according to the manufacturer's instructions. Unfold the paper as you smooth the border into place; do not place a cut edge directly in the corner, but 1 or 2 inches past it. Brush the edges of the border with a wallpaper brush or a dry paint roller to make sure they are secure.

To miter the corners (if the border goes around a window or door frame), overlap the ends of the two pieces and cut through both layers at a 45 degree angle; use a sharp utility knife and a straight edge. If you are using a border that has a distinctive motif, camouflage the mitered seam by cutting out a motif, then centering and pasting the motif over the seam.

- ❀ Mark off a border-sized strip where desired around the room and paint it a strong color. Then glue bits and pieces of swirled rope or colored cording to the painted area for a three-dimensional border.

- ❀ Stencil a decorative border or individual motifs on an otherwise plain wall. Precut stencils are readily available at craft stores. Once you get started, you'll think of many places where a stencil design will enhance the room. Consider stenciling around a window frame or chair rail, along the ceiling, on the ceiling, and around the doorways. Or you may see possible stenciling surfaces on a lampshade, on a bed frame, or on other pieces of furniture in the room. You may want to carry the stencil design onto the bed linens for a total look.

Fabric Magic

Cover your walls with fabric. This kind of wall covering is sometimes more desirable than the more traditional alternative, wallpaper. Why? Because it's totally removable and reusable! Select one of the several application methods that suits your needs the best. Start with only one wall. It's not as intimidating (and it's less expensive!). (See page 185 for two easy methods.)

☀ To cover any wall imperfections, gather fabric onto a rod, hang it at ceiling level, and let the fabric drape to the floor.

☀ Another alternative is to attach the fabric to hooks on the ceiling or wall with café rings and cup hooks.

☀ Other textiles such as quilts and rugs add visual interest, sound proofing, and warmth to any room. Hang, drape, and stack a variety of quilts throughout the room. (Refer to "Decorating with Quilts" in chapter 10 for more inspiration.)

☀ Suspend floor-length panels of fabric from pegs or cup hooks installed at the ceiling line. For added drama, allow the top edge of the fabric to hang loosely between the pegs for a swag effect. This looks best if the area to be covered is about $3/4$ as wide as the width of fabric you are using (e.g., 54-inch-wide fabric will cover $40^{1}/_{2}$ inches). Measure the width of the wall and divide it into even increments to determine where to place the pegs/cup hooks. Hem the top edge of each fabric panel with a double 2-inch hem; hem the bottom edge with a double 4-inch hem. Equally space and handstitch to the fabric the same number of small drapery rings as the number of hooks or pegs on the wall. Suspend the panels over the hooks.

Paint Strokes of Genius

Using a palette of wonderful colors plus some basic tools such as brushes, sponges, rags, feathers, and combs, you can help any room in your home undergo a magical metamorphosis.

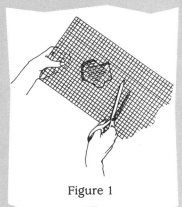

Figure 1

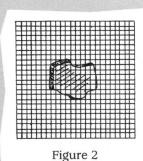

Figure 2

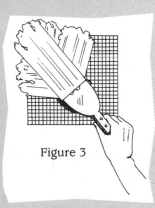

Figure 3

The Hole Story

Before taking on any painting or wallpapering job, you may need to repair a hole or two on the wall. Small holes can be repaired with Spackle (follow the directions on the package). However, large holes need more attention. Here is an easy way to repair holes that don't require filling in with pieces of drywall.

1. Remove any pieces of torn drywall with a utility knife.

2. Apply a self-adhesive mesh patch (fig. 1) over the hole (available in paint and hardware stores). Select a patch that is wide enough to cover the hole being repaired plus 1 inch or more beyond the edges all the way around (fig. 2).

3. Patch the prepared area with a thin coat of spackling paste applied with a putty knife. With a larger and wider putty knife, drag knife across spackling paste while applying light pressure (fig. 3). Paste should cover mesh and surface should be smooth. Allow to dry.

4. Sand the surface with a fine-grit sandpaper to remove any ridges and irregularities. Do not sand down to the patch. Wipe the area clean with a rag. Apply a second and possible third coat of paste as before, allowing each coat to dry completely before adding another coat.

5. Once the last coat is dry, sand the surface if necessary. Wipe the entire area clean of dust before painting. Cover the repaired area with primer before applying paint.

3 – Ceilings and Walls

☼ A way to use two different colors in a room is to paint your focus wall a deep tone and the remaining walls a lighter version of the same color.

☼ Want to paint adjoining rooms two different colors? Or every wall in the same room a different color? Go right ahead. The secret is to select colors that are the same value. Hold the paint-chip color cards side by side. Select colors from the same position on the card for superior results.

☼ Instead of trying to hide them, turn your decorating nightmares (exposed pipes, radiators, and even uneven ceilings) into "art objects" by painting them intense colors. Paint the remaining portions of the room with a coordinating color.

☼ Paint the trim in a room a color that contrasts with the walls. For even more drama, apply a faux finish such as a crackle or marbleized look. If you don't have molding in your home, consider installing some around the room. Crown moldings, baseboard moldings, and chair rails add architectural character to any room.

☼ Create dramatic diamonds in paint on the walls. Use two coordinating colors or two shades of the same color to create the design. (See page 194 for complete instructions for this project.)

☼ In general, you can expect 1 gallon of paint to cover from 350 to 400 square feet. However, check the label of the paint you select for the paint's spread rate (the square feet of surface each coat of paint will cover). Coverage will depend on the color of paint selected and the wall surface being painted.

☼ In case you need to repaint or touch up in the future, write specific information on the back of a switch plate in the room you are painting. The notations should include the brand name, the name of the paint color, the finish (flat, semi-gloss), the custom color formula if the paint was a special match, and the place and date where the paint was purchased. Without this information it may be difficult to match the original color and finish.

☼ Calculate paint quantities as closely as possible to avoid having leftovers and a paint-disposal dilemma. Keep a small amount of paint (in a sealable container) for touch-ups and then donate any leftover paint to theater groups, community centers, or a local shelter. It is best to store latex paint in glass or plastic containers; use metal cans for oil-base paint.

☼ Paint a mural on one wall. Use an opaque projector to project favorite vacation photographs onto the wall to give you guidance. Wall murals open up a room visually and eliminate the need to hang additional pictures on the wall.

☼ It's not difficult to earn your (painted) stripes on your walls. The stripes can be a combination of a flat and glossy paint or a flat and ragged finish. Use your imagination. Try a tri-color stripe technique. (See page 195 for complete instructions for this technique.)

☼ Before spending the time to stencil a whole room, do a "test pattern" first. Stencil the selected design on clear vinyl and position it around the room in various places with quick-release painter's tape. Live with the design for several days to make sure the color and design are what you want.

Before You Begin To Paint

- Remove all window coverings and hardware from the windows and any pictures and wall hangings from the wall.
- Roll up any carpets and cover them with plastic drop cloths.
- Cover any exposed flooring (or installed carpet) with drop cloths.
- Move all the furniture to the center of the room and cover it with drop cloths.
- Remove all switch and outlet plates.

Use the Right Paint

Two important considerations when selecting paint are the color and the sheen. The sheen will affect the look of the paint job and the paint performance as well. Keep these characteristics in mind when selecting the perfect paint for your job.

Flat Paint

- is good for general use on walls and ceilings

- hides surface imperfections

- is difficult to remove stains from

- is recommended for low-traffic areas

- is an excellent choice for living room and bedroom walls, ceilings, and hallways

Eggshell, Satin, or Low-Luster Paints

- have slightly more luster than flat paints

- resist stains better than flat paint

- can be used where a slight sheen is desired

- are recommended for kitchens, bathrooms, children's rooms, playrooms, hallways, and woodwork

Semi-Gloss Paint*

- is more stain resistant than eggshell or satin paints

- is easy-to-clean

- is excellent to use on surfaces that are subject to wear and frequent washings

- can be used on kitchen and bathroom walls, hallways, children's rooms, playrooms, doors, window trim, kitchen cabinets, shelves, banisters, and railings

Gloss Paint*

- is tougher and more durable and stain-resistant than paints with less sheen

- is easiest to clean

- is highly reflective and reveals surface imperfections more than other types of paint

- can be used for kitchen and bathroom walls, trim, window frames and sills, and door jams

---

* *These types of paints are also known as* enamels. *Enamel paints are the most stain resistant and easiest to wash of any interior paints.*

❋ The secret to successful stenciling is to apply the paint with an almost dry brush. After loading the brush with the desired color, dab the brush on paper towels until it's dry. Apply the paint to the cutout portion of the stencil with a light pounding or swirling motion.

❋ Sprinkle stencil motifs over the walls to create visual impact. Select a classic design such as a medallion and use a paint that is only slightly different from the background color for an elegant and sophisticated look. For example, be daring and paint the walls red and then stencil a design in a darker shade of red.

I CAN'T AFFORD WALLPAPER, AND I DON'T WANT PLAIN WALLS. WHAT CAN I DO?

❋ Stamping is another alternative to adding color to any wall. Select from a large assortment of precut stamped designs and specially formulated paint to create your design. The design is transferred to the wall by pressing the paint-covered stamp pad to the surface of the wall.

❋ To create your own wall stamp, all you need is 1/2-inch upholstery foam or a discarded mouse pad, cardboard, glue, and a utility knife. Decide on your design (refer to a coloring book) and enlarge it to the desired size on a copier. Cut out the enlarged design and glue it to the cardboard. Then glue the cardboard to foam and allow to dry overnight. Cut out the shape with a utility knife. Dip the stamp into latex or acrylic craft paint and press stamp to the wall.

❋ Create one-of-a-kind plaid walls with a roller that has been specially sculpted in various widths. (See page 193 for complete instructions.)

❋ If you love quilts but don't want to sew one from fabric, paint a simple geometric quilt directly onto the wall. (See page 196 to learn how.)

❋ If you want to develop a truly unique wall design, consider doing freehand painting. Designs can vary from geometrics to doodles to realistic images.

❋ Are you a little nervous about painting freehand on a wall? Before embarking on such a project, try this: practice painting on the wall using a paintbrush dipped only in water. When you feel confident, dip the brush in paint.

3 – Ceilings and Walls

❋ Paint dark wood paneling a new and refreshing color. Thoroughly wash the surface with a powdered cleanser such as TSP (do not use a liquid spray cleanser as it may leave a soapy film). Prime the surface with a 100 percent acrylic primer sealer. Then finish with two coats of latex paint in a color of your choice. Note: Paneling will soak up a lot of primer; you may need to apply two coats. Select the best quality primer that your budget allows.

❋ Revigorate old wooden kitchen cabinets in much the same way—by painting! Remove the doors from the frames and remove any hardware. Wash the cabinets and frames. Lightly sand any surfaces that will show and remove any dust with a tack cloth or a rag dipped in mineral spirits. Apply an acrylic primer sealer (select one that is formulated for kitchens if possible) to all wood surfaces (including the frame). Then apply semi-gloss paint in the color of your choice; allow the surface to dry. Replace the doors and the hardware.

❋ If you have severely cracked walls, rip ordinary brown kraft paper (or brown paper bags) into large, irregular, square pieces. Crumple the pieces, then smooth them out for added texture. Apply the pieces to cover the entire wall with the kind of paste used for strippable vinyl wallpaper. Paint the wall in a color of your choice (you may also apply a more subtle faux finish such as "ragging on"). Use a rubber stamp of your choice to apply metallic paint to the paper (do not pick a stamp with an intricate design). Seal the entire wall with a tinted, oil-base glaze.

Stripe Out

Add energy to any room of your home by incorporating stripes into your decorating scheme. Stripes can make a room more playful, tranquil, elegant, dramatic, and romantic.

❋ When picking stripes for walls (either wallpaper or painted stripes), use colors that complement, rather than fight, each other. For example, beige and cream are perfect harmonious colors.

☼ A subtle striped wall covering provides the perfect background for antique mirrors or your favorite pieces of art.

☼ Wide stripes provide architectural interest to an otherwise plain wall. Narrow stripes have a more subtle effect.

☼ Vertical stripes enhance the height of the room. But be careful. Narrow stripes can create a closed-in feeling. Use starkly contrasting stripes with care. For example, installing them below a chair rail will avoid visual distraction. Stripes with lots of space between them are easier on the eye.

☼ Pin stripes may create a "jumpy" feeling in a room; a wider stripe is more settling to the eye.

☼ Use a complementary wallpaper border to visually stop the stripe at the top of the wall if there is no molding.

☼ Stripes are a good choice to use in a child's room. They create a sense of order in what may be a chaotic scene.

☼ Don't be shy about mixing stripes and flowers in one room because stripes will alleviate the "flower power" of an all-floral room.

☼ Color washed stripes are easy to do yourself! Simply mark off the width of the stripes and sponge on a latex paint/glaze combination. (See page 194 to learn how.)

Paneling Update

WHAT CAN I
DO WITH UGLY
PANELING?

Ugly wall paneling is a common problem. The solution is easier than you might think.

☼ Thoroughly clean the surface of the wood paneling with a powdered cleanser such as TSP or a biodegradable alternative to remove any old wax, residues left by cleaning products, or wood preservatives that may have been applied to the paneling. Work from the bottom to the top of the wall, rinse, and let the surface dry.

☼ If your paneling has a shiny surface, use 100-grit sandpaper to scuff the surface. Remove any dust and wipe the walls clean with a tack cloth and/or a rag dampened with mineral spirits.

3 – Ceilings and Walls

☀ Prime the entire surface with a primer made specifically for paneling; use a roller with a 3/8-inch nap. Consult your local paint professional for the perfect primer for your paneling.

☀ Allow the primer to dry completely and then fill in any nail holes, unwanted grooves, or distress marks with wood putty. When the putty dries, sand the surface smooth. Another alternative is to use a lightweight Spackle. This product does not normally need to be sanded after use and paint can usually be applied shortly after filling the holes.

☀ Use latex paint in the color of your choice to give old paneling a new lease on life; use a 3/8-inch nap roller to apply the paint. You will need two coats of paint to ensure even coverage.

☀ For special effects, sponge or rag roll over an opaque basecoat. For an even more textural effect, use a flat interior latex paint as the basecoat and use a rag or sponge to apply a coat of semi-gloss.

Faux/Real

Release your adventurous spirit by trying one of the many faux finish painting techniques. There is no such thing as a mistake—so dive in and have fun! Keep in mind that the techniques are closer to an art than a science. In other words, the most spectacular results are made by experimenting, not by following a rigid formula. Try color washing, combing, sponging, ragging, dragging, spattering, veining, stippling, crosshatching, combing, or marbleizing.

Color washing is a translucent effect that is achieved when paint is thinned and brushed over wood or a painted surface. To produce a subtle texture, remove some of the color wash with cheesecloth.

Combing uses a notched tool made of rubber or cardboard that is dragged across a just-painted surface to create imperfect stripes, plaids, waves, or squares. (See page 197 for complete instructions.)

Crosshatching involves the application of several coats of a translucent glaze applied in a crisscrossed pattern over a basecoat. Repeat the crosshatched pattern with a different-colored glaze. (See page 197 for instructions.)

Dragging results in a striated effect and is achieved when the tip of a very stiff brush or a piece of steel wool is dragged across a wet surface.

Glazing combines paint and a glazing liquid. Glazing liquid is available in a matte or glossy finish. Any mixture that is more than half glaze results in a more transparent look. A mixture that is less than half glazing liquid is more opaque. Experiment to find the look you want. Apply this paint/glaze mixture to a previously painted surface with a mitt, sponge, or brush. Special effects can be achieved by dragging a window washer's squeegee with "teeth" across the glazed surface.

Marbling includes adding veins to a textured surface with an artist's brush and then softening the lines with a feather or sponge.

Ragging-on uses a rag to apply a color wash to the wall. Ragging-off is a technique that uses a bunched-up piece of fabric to remove a color wash.

Smooshing is a technique using a plastic drop cloth or plastic bag. The plastic is crumpled and then dabbed or rubbed on a freshly painted surface to create texture.

Spattering is a messy but fun faux finishing technique. Dip a stiff paintbrush (or toothbrush) into paint. Then rub your finger across the bristles and paint will spatter on the wall in a random pattern.

Sponging creates a mottled effect when a natural sponge dipped into a contrasting color is pressed in a random pattern over the wall.

Stippling uses the tip of a brush "stabbed" repeatedly onto a wet surface to create tiny pin pricks.

Woodgraining uses special tools that are dragged through a glaze to simulate woodgrain.

Painting Primer

Here's everything you need to know for a successful paint job. These tips will insure that your painting project will look as good as if you hired a professional.

- Repair any cracks or other flaws before beginning. If you have a plaster wall and the cracks are large and the surface has buckled, remove any old plaster by digging out the area surrounding the cracks.

- Work spackling compound into any holes or cracks with a flexible putty knife. Let it dry thoroughly. If you have larger holes, refer to "The Hole Story" on page 31.

- Sand the surface smooth. Clean up any lingering dust or dirt.

- If your walls have been previously painted, lightly sand glossy areas and clean greasy areas thoroughly.

- Once surface repairs are made, clean the walls thoroughly; use TSP (or a biodegradable alternative). Wash the walls from the ground up; this prevents streaks. Allow them to dry thoroughly.

- If your walls have never been painted (such as new dry-wall), tape and fill all panel joints. When applying a lighter color over a darker color, use a primer sealer tinted to a lighter shade of the selected top coat color to ensure even coverage. Use the best primer that you can afford; it will save time and paint. A primer does two things: (1) seals the surface so stains and the original paint color will not show through and (2) promotes adhesion so the top coat won't peel.

- Before beginning a painting project, rub your hands with baby oil to help remove the paint from your hands afterwards.

- Select the best paint that your budget allows. Try your best to stay away from cheap paint—even though the price is inviting—and take advantage of good paint on sale if you can. Cheap paint lacks the body of good-quality paint; it's thin and runny. Cheap paint does not offer the best coverage, so more than likely you'll have to apply several coats. (That translates into more work and more paint!)

- To eliminate the drip of paint over the sides of the paint can, remove the lid and use an ice pick to make holes around the rim of the can. The holes should be made in the deepest groove and spaced about 1 inch apart. The paint will drip back into the can through the holes. This step will prevent overflowing, save paint, and keep the can clean.

- If the project you are working on requires more than one can of paint, painting professionals recommend mixing all of the paint into one large container. This will assure that the color and sheen will be consistent in the room.

- Dip the brush into the paint no more than halfway. Tap the brush gently against the side of the can to remove excess paint. Do not wipe the brush across the lip of the can.

- Paint the ceiling first. If the ceiling is going to be a different color from the walls, use a brush or edging tool to apply paint around the edges where the ceiling and wall meet.

- Rollers with extension handles are great for painting ceilings. By using an extension handle, you may not need a ladder or scaffolding. However, keep a stepladder handy for painting corners and around the edge of the ceiling with a brush.

Continued

- If you use a roller, begin by painting an M shape. Then fill in with parallel horizontal strokes and finish with light vertical roller strokes. For best results, make your strokes as long and continuous as possible and roll into the wet surface to eliminate lap marks.

- After the ceiling is completely painted, paint the trim; use an angled brush for precise coverage. Use low-tack painter's tape on the wall around the window and door frames for a neat paint job.

- Use a brush or other edge-painting tool to outline any windows or doors in the wall color selected. Also paint the corners of each room before the largest part of the wall. This is called "cutting in." However, don't cut in the entire room before painting the walls; cut in as you progress around the room. This avoids the possibility of "hat banding," previously painted areas that show through the second coat as slightly darker bands near the ceiling.

- If painting with a brush, apply the first strokes in a sweeping arc pattern and then fill in with finishing strokes that are applied horizontally or vertically in the same direction.

- To save clean-up time when working on a large painting project, remove as much paint as possible from your brush, wrap it in plastic wrap and foil, and store it in the freezer so it retains its shape. The brush can be reused (with the same paint) without cleaning the brush thoroughly after each use. When you use the brush again, remove the plastic and foil and bring the brush to room temperature before using.

- Select the right paintbrush for the type of paint you are using. Natural bristle brushes are made to use with oil-based paints while synthetic brushes are a perfect match for latex paints.

- Clean bristle brushes with solvent. Work the solvent through the bristles into the center of the brush and down under the ferrule (metal band).

- Synthetic brushes can be cleaned with warm water and a mild soap; do not soak.

4 Windows of Opportunity

Window treatments aren't what they used to be! Gone are the days when windows could only be covered with pleats of fabric or plain roller shades. Today everything from bottles to wooden spoons to hankies can adorn the windows of your world.

Cures for the Common Curtain

If you want to try an unusual window treatment, here are some creative ideas to get you started.

☀ For a nontraditional window treatment, hand paint designs onto each window pane; use water-based or tempera paints. When you want to change these temporary designs, simply scrape off the old design and repaint.

☀ Light and airy window treatments can be created with generous amounts of gauzy fabric. Drape the fabric over a rod and around the window and hold it in place with tieback holders in fanciful shapes, ribbons, or satin cording.

☀ Many pieces of wide ribbon or lace draped over a decorative pole creates an attractive and unique window treatment.

☀ Train a potted ivy plant to climb up and around a window frame; use clear tacks to help guide the vine. If you need to, fill in gaps with silk ivy.

4 – Windows of Opportunity

✺ Customize a window by adding an etched (frosted) design around the edges. Select a design that complements your decorating style. Use etching cream (readily available in craft stores) and precut stencils to create your design. If you want to be more adventurous, cut your own design from self-adhesive vinyl shelf paper. Remember that the design has to be reversed to be etched. That is, cut away the area to be etched and leave the remaining background area intact when applying etching cream. The open areas create the design.

✺ Drape lace napkins or hankies over a curtain rod for a very feminine valance.

✺ Mount a decorative rod above a window. Hang a square tablecloth over the rod and cinch it with a coordinating ribbon at each side.

✺ A pair of pillowcases can be transformed in minutes to café curtains. Attach one edge of the pillowcase to a decorative rod with decorative clips (available where curtain hardware is sold). If your pillowcases have a decorative edge, consider the placement of this feature when planning this window treatment.

✺ Instead of a fabric window treatment, intersperse small paintings and glass plates inside individual window panes.

✺ Install several glass shelves inside the window frame and display colorful glasses, bowls, and vases.

✺ Drape a square lace tablecloth or several napkins diagonally over a decorative rod. Look in consignment shops for some interesting table linens.

✺ Place grapevines (available in craft stores) over arched windows; allow them to drape as they please for a natural decorating effect.

✺ Hang old cooking utensils with clear fishing line from a decorative rod in the kitchen. Your grandma's cupboard might contain some perfect items for this idea.

✺ Suspend a thin wire across the width of the window and from it hang a multitude of glass prisms. Use small screw eyes to hold the wire in place.

HOW CAN I DECORATE MY WINDOWS WHEN I DON'T SEW?

- Cut a length of picket fence to fit the top portion of a sashed window and mount it (points down) from the top of the window frame. Embellish the fence with dried or silk flowers or even garden-inspired stamps or stencils.

- Tack a lacy or colorful apron over a kitchen window and let the ties cascade down along each side.

- Use your hat collection as a valance. An added benefit of this treatment is that the hats can be changed to suit the season. (See page 200 for complete instructions for this project.)

- Paint, stencil, or stamp your otherwise plain molding with whimsical designs or favorite motifs. Hang a piece of fabric that features the same motifs inside the window frame.

- For seasonal decorating, use a valance over side curtains in the fall and winter. In the spring and summer, replace the side curtains with lace or sheers or remove them altogether.

Valances: Topping It Off

Valances are so simple to make! They are just enough alone, or they can be layered over matching or coordinating curtains, blinds, shades, and interior shutters.

- If you can sew a straight line, you can create terrific valances. Add decorator details such as tassels, covered buttons, cording, and trim for a custom look.

- Most valances require a minimal amount of fabric; however, do not skimp on the needed fullness. A general guideline is to make a rod pocket valance $2\frac{1}{2}$ to 3 times the width of the distance you are covering.

- Install the rod approximately 2 to 4 inches out from the outside edge of the window frame and 2 to 4 inches above the top edge of the window frame (wall studs usually surround the window frame). For best results, install the hardware before planning your window treatment so you can take accurate measurements.

4 – *Windows of Opportunity*

❀ Details do make a difference. Select hardware and trim to complement the valance style.

❀ Valances should be approximately 1/3 the length of the window. You may want to cut a large piece of paper the length you think you want your valance to be. Attach the paper to the rod with tape and step back to see if the length is pleasing to your eye.

❀ Line your valance with appropriate lining fabric. Use a white lining on all of your window treatments for a unified look from the outside of the house. Lined valances hang better and the lining acts as a protective layer to keep the sun from damaging your decorator fabric.

Blind Faith

Long known as a perfect undertreatment, with a little creativity blinds can hold their own as solo window decorations.

❀ Using acrylic paint in a contrasting color, sponge paint inexpensive vertical or horizontal blinds to add texture and color to your room.

❀ If the room you are decorating lacks a view, paint or stencil ordinary blinds with an outdoor theme.

❀ Horizontal mini-blinds can be brought to life by adding designs cut from adhesive-backed paper (such as Con-Tact brand paper) to the surface. Or create your own stick-on designs by applying a double-sided adhesive to the wrong side of patterned paper or fabric. Cut out shapes and apply to the surface of the blind.

❀ Room-darkening roller blinds (or shades) are a perfect undertreatment for a window treatment. Not only do they darken the room, but they give privacy and offer a layer of insulation.

❀ Roller blinds are perfect for small windows because they are not overwhelming and they allow a lot of natural light in when they are rolled up completely.

What's Your Exposure?

How your home is situated can affect your decorating choices.

- East-facing windows admit bright morning light into the room. Select sheer curtains or pull-down shades to soften the early morning rays.

- North-facing windows may need insulated shades under your planned or existing window treatments to conserve energy and keep out winter chills.

- South-facing windows gather sunlight all year round. Protect fine furnishings from sun damage with vertical blinds or pleated shades.

- Western-facing windows take in the afternoon sun. Again, protection is the key concern. Vertical blinds, pleated shades, or wooden shutters offer this layer of needed protection. Some companies offer shades that are solar powered—they are sun-sensitive and will automatically close when the sunlight becomes too strong.

☀ Place blinds inside the window frame to show off any decorative molding that surrounds the window.

☀ You can make your own fabric-covered roller blinds by using a special fusible shade material found in fabric stores. You can be even more creative and add a decoratively shaped hem along the bottom edge.

☀ Unroll a vinyl-coated window shade the length of the window. Prime the surface with a latex primer followed by the first coat of latex paint in a color of your choice. Tape diamond-shaped outlines to the surface with masking tape. Paint alternating diamonds in a coordinating color. Allow the shade to dry overnight, remove the tape, and install the shade in the window.

☀ When window shades become torn, save the hardware (the roller and slat). Replace the shade with an inexpensive plastic tablecloth that will complement the room. Hem the bottom of the shade to fit the slat with machine stitching, staples, double-sided tape, or glue. (Hide the stitching or staple line on the front side by gluing decorative trimming or ribbon over it.) Staple or tape the top edge of the new shade to the roller.

❀ An easy lacing technique using eyelets, decorative cording, a curtain rod, and a dowel is all that's needed to create a unique blind. (See page 176 for complete instructions.)

❀ A fun variation to the traditional blind is a "stagecoach roller shade." This shade rolls up from the bottom edge and is held in place with ribbons stitched to the front and back of the shade at the top edge. (See page 176 for complete instructions for this project.)

Window Whimsy

Decorating windows can be a challenge. However, after you review the following suggestions, your only challenge will be to decide which idea to use first.

❀ Utilize those beautiful decorative stitching patterns available on embroidery sewing machines to create one-of-a-kind fabrics from which your window treatment can be made. A distinguished motif embroidered onto a sheer fabric would be most elegant!

❀ You can also use machine embroidered designs to spruce up ready-made curtains or valances. Simply stitch a border along the hem or under the rod pocket to create a personalized window statement.

❀ Use printed and solid ready-made sheer curtains on the same rod for a creative and quick window treatment. Place printed sheers toward the center of the window with coordinating solid sheers to the outside edges.

❀ If you can't find printed sheers to coordinate with your color scheme, it's easy to create your own. Simply cut a sponge into any shape you would like, dip it into fabric paint, and stamp it onto plain sheer fabric. Before stamping the fabric, blot the dipped sponge on paper towels to remove excess paint and ensure a crisper impression of your design.

☀ Hang three pairs of ready-made sheers on the same rod. Loosely braid the three panels together (the way you braid hair), and let the braids hang down on each side of the window. Use any color combination you want. Secure the ends of the braids with cording or decorative ribbon.

☀ Make your own sheer curtains. Hem all four sides of two lengths of sheer fabric. Then add ribbon tabs along the top edge. For added embellishment, stitch or fuse ribbon in a decorative pattern over the surface of the curtains. (See page 178 for complete directions for this project.)

☀ Combine shutters and lightweight fabric curtains for a cozy, yet private, window treatment.

☀ Use a luxurious fabric for window treatments to compensate for a lack of architectural interest in a room.

☀ An inexpensive alternative to costly trims is to buy beaded Christmas garlands. Simply drape the multitudes of beads over an existing window treatment for a unique look.

☀ In place of a fabric valance, use a wooden or Styrofoam cornice board; several different kits are available in decorating centers. Paint, stipple, stencil, or antique the board, or cover it with fabric. Other ideas for personalizing a cornice board include adding decoupage designs cut from inexpensive wrapping paper or applying a wallpaper border (or portions of a border) to the front and sides of the cornice board.

☀ Winterize the look of your decor by adding some coziness during cold weather. Install a spring-tension curtain rod in the window and hang colorful mittens and gloves from it with small drapery clips. This is a great way to utilize the mittens that are missing their mates.

☀ Custom-made stained glass designs can be quite costly but are wonderful alternatives to traditional window treatments. You can simulate the look of stained glass quite successfully by using a specially formulated liquid glass paint and "leading" (available in craft stores). Add a design to the entire window surface just around the edge.

Common-Sense Care for Curtains

Once you have chosen your curtains, take good care of them. By caring for them properly, years will be added to their life.

- Washing window treatments is not recommended if decorator fabric was used in their construction. These fabrics should be dry cleaned. Try to keep curtains as dust-free as possible to prevent the need for frequent cleaning.

- Vacuum, dust, or shake curtains regularly to remove loose dirt and dust. Pay particular attention to pleats and gathers, where dust collects.

- Hang your window treatments outside on a dry, breezy day to help keep the fabrics clean and fresh. Alternatively, place a curtain panel and a damp—not wet—cloth into the dryer. Set the dryer on "air fluff" and tumble the curtain for about 15 minutes. The tumbling action shakes out the dirt and dust.

- If you dry clean your window treatments, be aware that some of the protective fabric finishes may be removed during the cleaning process. This may result in the fabrics' being less crisp and losing some of their protection against stains or sunlight. Ask friends or a local decorator for recommendations about good dry cleaners. Keep a record of the finished size, fabric finishes, fiber content, and manufacturer's care instructions for your window treatments and provide your dry cleaner with this information.

- Some window treatments, such as those used in a kitchen, are more likely to become stained and soiled. Select fabrics for these areas that are washable, shrink resistant, and colorfast.

- If you must wash curtains, wash them in small loads; crowding will cause wrinkling.

- To wash lace or sheer curtains, place them in a mesh bag or pillow-case, or if they are especially delicate, wash them by hand.

- If the window treatments are the same size in the same room, rotate them periodically from window to window. Because different windows get different amounts of sun exposure, this technique prevents one treatment from wearing out or fading before another.

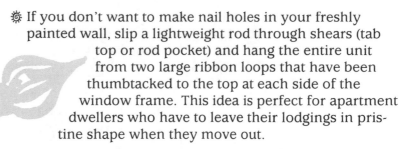

☀ If you don't want to make nail holes in your freshly painted wall, slip a lightweight rod through shears (tab top or rod pocket) and hang the entire unit from two large ribbon loops that have been thumbtacked to the top at each side of the window frame. This idea is perfect for apartment dwellers who have to leave their lodgings in pristine shape when they move out.

☀ Drape a garland of silk flowers seductively over lace or sheer curtains for a very romantic window treatment.

☀ Hang lace curtain panels from a tension rod and then place hankies over the rod to create a simple valance.

☀ Team inexpensive sheers with a beautiful piece of tapestry as a valance. The contrasting textures add lots of sophistication and flair.

☀ Stretch picture wire tightly across a window to serve as a rod and then install grommets in a lightweight piece of fabric to create a valance. To hang a valance from the grommets, use curtain hooks or simply thread the wire through the grommets before hanging the valance.

☀ Wrap and loop layers and layers of lace over a curtain rod. Intertwine silk flowers, tiny white Christmas lights, and vines with the lace for a romantic look.

☀ Create a window scarf by cutting a length of fabric or lace and tapering each end. Add some decorative fringe to one long edge and both diagonal edges. Make rings of ribbon or fabric. To attach the scarf to the rod, use lengths of ribbons or fabrics as tabs and use them in place of swag rings. Insert the length of fabric through the tabs; space tabs evenly across length of window and drape the fabric between the tabs in attractive folds.

☀ If windows are different shapes and sizes within the same room, use treatments that are similar in style for a unified look.

☀ If windows are of different heights, install all the rods at the same point on the wall to give the illusion that the windows are the same height.

4 – Windows of Opportunity

❁ To customize ready-made curtains, try one of these ideas. Sew or fuse a wide band of fabric around the perimeter of the curtains, paint the fabric with fabric paints, add buttons in an allover design, or stitch or fuse trims to the edges.

❁ When planning a window treatment for a child's room, keep the design simple and practical. A shirred valance over a colorful shade may be all you need.

❁ Add some flair to existing Roman shades to give them a new lease on life. Stencil or paint small designs all over the fabric; sew colorful buttons in a random pattern; tie bows or knots into fabric scraps, ribbon, lace, or even burlap and stitch them to the surface; top the shade with a new valance or a fabric-covered cornice.

❁ Sometimes the best window treatment is none at all. Of course, you have to consider how much privacy is needed before you "undress" your window. Many times, windows in the living room, kitchen, and dining room can be left untreated. If your windows have special architectural details, consider letting these features speak for themselves. Another time when you may opt to use nothing on a window is if a window treatment could actually take away from an interior or exterior view.

❁ If you have a window that looks out over a garden or a wonderful view, but you can't leave it completely bare, use a window treatment made from light and airy fabric such as lace or organdy.

Creative Hardware

Hardware—once hidden—has become an important design feature in window treatments. Choose from the large selection of rods, finials, and poles now available in home improvement stores to create your own.

❁ Bamboo poles or even tree branches bring a little of the outdoors indoors and are perfect to hang curtains from.

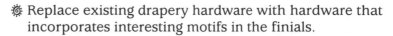

☀ Replace existing drapery hardware with hardware that incorporates interesting motifs in the finials.

☀ Make your own curtain rod from twigs, boat oars, fishing poles, tennis rackets, hockey sticks, rakes, or fireplace tools. Drape fabric from the newly fashioned hardware.

☀ Transform wooden pole rods and finials into custom pieces by sponging them with paint, dyeing or staining them with fabric dye, adding a crackle or marble finish, or adding metallic accents. Or cover a rod and finials with scraps of leftover fabric to coordinate with the rest of the room.

☀ Spray-paint wrought-iron rods and finials gold, silver, or copper for a touch of opulence.

☀ Copper piping makes an inexpensive curtain rod. It's available at your local hardware store and can be cut into the exact length you need.

☀ Gather together doorknobs or smaller drawer or cabinet knobs and install them evenly over a window. These items make interesting items to drape tab curtains from.

Terrific Tiebacks

You can add personality to a room with just the tiebacks you select. Consider using some of these ideas for quick, easy, and inexpensive accents.

☀ Tie floor-length curtains back with colorful bandannas or scarves.

☀ Mount horseshoes to the wall and drape the curtains over and through the U-shaped openings.

☀ String tiny flowerpots (available in craft stores) as you would pearls. Tie knots inside and outside of the opening in the pots to prevent them from sliding. Before stringing them, decorate the pots with paint, decals, or fabric.

☀ Use your old belts (or ones found in discount or second-hand stores) as unexpected tiebacks.

☀ For a romantic room, use ribbon streamers attached to nosegays of dried or silk flowers as tiebacks.

Suggested Placements for Tiebacks

Sill-Length

Floor-length curtains or drapes fall into graceful curves if the tiebacks are placed at the height of the sill.

Placed Low

By placing tiebacks low (about 2/3 of the way down from the top of the curtains), an illusion of a tall, narrow window is created. This effect will obscure light because more of the window is covered by the curtains.

Placed High

To create an illusion of height, place the tiebacks about 1/3 of the way down from the top. This effect will also let in the most light.

Sill-Length

Placed Low

Placed High

- ☀ Elegant tapestry ribbons trimmed with gold braid and tassels are perfect for tiebacks.

- ☀ Embellish your curtains with elements from nature such as grapevine wreaths, pine cones, straw, willows, seashells, or sprays of wheat.

- ☀ Ropes of fake pearls used alone or intertwined with gold beads are nontraditional, yet romantic and elegant, tiebacks.

- ☀ Paper fans (found in party stores or Asian shops around the country and abroad) can be attached to curtains with thick silk-like cording for an interesting tieback.

- ☀ Stiffened crocheted doilies gathered into rosettes and trimmed with satin-cord streamers can adorn lace, sheer, or otherwise plain curtains. Fabric stiffener can be found in craft stores.

5 Furniture

urniture not only has to fit its designated room, but it must fit your life as well. You can shop at a furniture store for a whole suite of furniture or scour flea markets and antique malls for some special finds.

Making Arrangements

The most inexpensive way—in fact, it's free—to change the look of any room is to rearrange the furniture. Here are some suggestions.

❀ Consider moving the furniture away from the walls and grouping several pieces together for an intimate conversation area. To encourage conversation, don't place the seats more than 8 feet apart. To save your back, sketch new room arrangements on graph paper before you actually move the furniture.

❀ Changing the arrangement of the furniture can give a room a totally new look. If you can't decide if you like the way a room is arranged, have a few people over for an informal gathering. After they leave, observe how your guests rearranged the furniture in the room. Can you identify small conversation areas? Was other furniture brought into the room? Perhaps you should consider these "suggestions" when trying to improve a room's overall comfort.

5 – Furniture

☀ If your bedroom window provides a wonderful view, arrange your bed so you can look out your window when you wake up in the morning.

☀ Rearrange your kitchen table and chairs so they are close to a window so you can watch the world wake up while having your morning coffee.

☀ For a seasonal change, rearrange your furniture so that it faces the window with the prettiest view instead of the fireplace.

☀ For a bedroom with limited wall space, place the bed at an angle in one corner. Then make the bed the focal point of the room. Add a canopy, use a quilt as the main bedcover, and don't forget to pile on the pillows!

☀ Placing furniture against the walls around the perimeter of the room is not your only option. If this dance-floor style no longer appeals to you, try bringing the furniture closer together in the middle of the room with accent pieces radiating out from this central point.

☀ Combine furniture made from all different materials (wicker, metal, wood, and so on) and unify the grouping with fabrics of a similar color scheme.

☀ The most interesting piece of furniture for a bedroom is an old-fashioned dressing table. Add a lace skirt, top the table with glass, then display a framed mirror, perfume bottles, and a beautiful comb-and-brush set.

☀ A corner cupboard will enlarge your capacity for displaying your favorite collectibles.

☀ When decorating a room that will be occupied primarily by men, select large, comfortable furniture pieces.

☀ Instead of a traditional low coffee table placed in front of the sofa, use a small drop-leaf parlor table. This higher surface is more accessible—especially when entertaining. This arrangement works best if the seating arrangement is two-sided (for example, an L shape).

☀ Place a comfortable chair in the corner of a foyer or hallway. Add a small table, a lamp, and some pretty flowers to create a warm welcome for your guests.

☀ A "collection" of small 18-to-24-inch-high tables near a sofa can be used for casual dining and entertaining.

Finishing Touches

Many times a perfect piece of furniture is what makes a room look complete. You might find a wonderful piece at a flea market or add some excitement to a piece of furniture you already own.

☀ Add a fabric-covered or decoratively painted folding screen to any corner of the room. This colorful addition can serve double duty—to be decorative and to camouflage unattractive areas of the room.

☀ Have you ever heard of "hobo art"? It's fun and quite inexpensive. Paint the surface of a wooden piece of furniture, then cover the surface with a variety of soda pop caps from bottles. Glue the caps in place with a hot glue gun.

WHAT CAN I DO WITH MY FLEA MARKET FIND?

☀ Decoupage a motif cut from wallpaper or fabric onto a piece of furniture to tie the furniture and decor together.

☀ Piece wallpaper scraps together to create quilt blocks on the front door of a pie chest or cabinet.

☀ Decorate the front of a chest of drawers with three-dimensional plaster-like compound such as Aleene's 3D Accents Design Paste (available in craft stores). This versatile compound can be used with stencils or applied freehand to create your own design.

5 – Furniture

☀ Give new life to any scratched piece of furniture by applying broken pieces of pottery, dishes, tile, or colored glass to the surface and then filling in between them with grout. (See page 206 for instructions.)

☀ Decorative wallpaper borders applied to the perimeter of a tired tabletop give an entirely new look to an otherwise dated furniture piece. (See page 202 for instructions.)

High-Style Headboards

What's behind your bed? If you need an idea for a different headboard, try one of these.

☀ An interesting, yet inexpensive, headboard can be created by painting a horizontal rectangle on the wall where the bed will be placed. Frame the rectangle with decorative molding. Leave the painted area solid, or stencil a design, apply a faux finish, or decorate with wallpaper cutouts or decals. You may want to extend the "headboard" along the wall by adding a coordinated wallpaper border horizontally from each side of the headboard. Add the same molding along the top and bottom edges of the border for accent purposes.

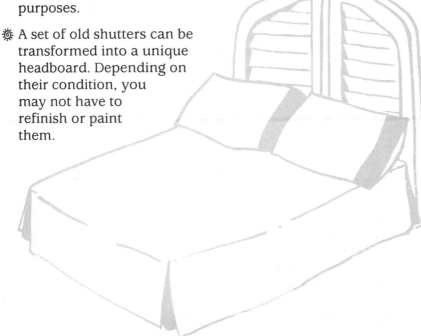

☀ A set of old shutters can be transformed into a unique headboard. Depending on their condition, you may not have to refinish or paint them.

❀ A unique headboard can be made by framing a piece of lattice with molding. Before attaching the unit to a wall, staple a piece of fabric to the backside of the frame. Add silk flowers and vines to the slats of the lattice for an instant garden.

❀ A pair of woolen blankets folded and hung together over a rod hung up behind a bed is a wonderfully inexpensive headboard.

❀ Cover a hollow door with batting and fabric to create an inexpensive headboard for a king-sized bed. To mount the headboard, insert screw eyes at each end on the back of the board and hang it like a picture frame or mirror.

❀ For a soft and romantic look, mount decorative hardware behind a bed and drape layers of lace or another sheer fabric (and maybe a little ribbon) over it.

❀ Add some dimension to a wall-painted headboard with rope and stenciled three-dimensional shapes. Simply draw the shape of the headboard directly on the wall. Paint the ropes an interesting color. Then nail two lengths of rope, side by side, directly over the sketched lines. Use a three-dimensional plasterlike compound such as Aleene's 3D Accents Design Paste to stencil the selected design inside the headboard area. Allow to dry. Paint the inside of the headboard, including the stenciled area. This technique could also be adapted for wall borders.

Something from Nothing

❀ Transform an old card table into a colorful kitchen table by painting the legs a fresh, new color. Make a table cover out of an exciting-looking fabric.

❀ Use door shutters to create a folding screen. Then add shelves at different heights on all three shutters. Shelves can easily be made with brackets and 1-inch by 6-inch pine shelving. (Page 200 in chapter 19 will show you how to assemble the screen and add shelves.)

❀ Make a twin bed into a daybed by placing one long edge against the wall. Use two king-sized bed pillows against the wall and fill in any empty spots with a collection of interesting throw pillows.

5 – Furniture

❂ An old, worn window can be transformed into a pot rack for the kitchen by hanging it horizontally from the ceiling with strong hooks and chains. Select a sturdy window and reinforce the corners with corner brackets. Install ceiling hooks on the underside of the window from which to hang pots.

❂ Glue hardback books together in a stack to the height of an end table. Top with a stained or painted wooden disk. For a low coffee table, stack smaller books into four "legs" and top them with a rectangular piece of glass.

❂ Create a three-dimensional faux bookshelf with wall borders and decorative molding. Select a wall border with a design of books lined up as if standing on end on a bookshelf. Determine what size "bookshelf" you want and mark the wall for placement. Cut the border and the molding into strips the desired length of the "shelves." Install the wall border; follow manufacturer's instructions. Allow space between the strips of border to install molding. Paint or stain the molding to match your decor. Install a molding strip below each row of books to look like a shelf. Add vertical side pieces of molding to both sides of the bookshelf. To finish, add a more substantial piece of molding to indicate the top edge of the unit.

❂ Transform an otherwise dull bookshelf or knickknack shelf into one of the most colorful pieces of furniture in your home. Simply paint the inside of each compartment or cubbyhole a different color. To create cohesiveness, select colors of the same value and paint any exposed front edges one color. Use latex paint because it cleans up easily with water.

❂ Bring a piece of outdoor furniture inside. Wicker, wrought iron, or weathered wood adds instant personality to any room.

☼ Replace torn webbing on an outdoor chair with a colorful fabric seat and back. Bring it inside for extra seating. (Learn how to do this project on page 204.)

☼ Old steamer trunks, pine crates, mismatched suitcases, even a concrete birdbath can be transformed into unique coffee and end tables.

☼ Create an inexpensive, yet attractive, desk for your home office by using two, 2-drawer filing cabinets and a plywood board or hollow door as the desk surface. Spray the filing cabinets with a stonelike finish (available in craft and hardware stores). Paint the desk surface in a coordinating color, or try your hand at a faux finishing technique. (Refer to page 38 for painting ideas.) If you like, create separate file cabinet "fronts" and attach them directly to the front of each file cabinet drawer. You may need to attach new drawer pulls to accommodate the added thickness of the drawer fronts.

☼ Create a sophisticated set of table and chairs for your kitchen by using inexpensive folding lawn chairs. (Buy them at summer's end for even more savings.) Make a table from a square wooden base and use a plywood circle as a tabletop. No one will ever know the table is not real—simply cover the table with a floor-length fabric table skirt.

☼ Mismatched chairs will look good together if they are all stained or painted to match. Make simple chair cushions from the same fabric to create the illusion of a matched set.

☼ Change the knobs on a chest of drawers for a quick facelift. Select from porcelain or brass styles available in hardware stores. Or paint wooden knobs in colors of your

Easy Fireplace Screen

Create a fireplace screen from a discarded cardboard cutting board. (New ones are inexpensive and available at fabric stores.) This gridded board is already folded, and it is a good height for a fireplace screen. Remember, these fireplace screens are not fireproof and should only be used in the off-season for decorative purposes.

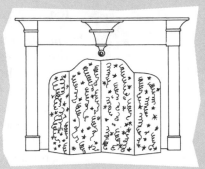

1. Remove sections if necessary to fit your own fireplace opening. Once the board is the size you want, you can create a decorative top edge on the screen panels. Trace a shape on each panel and then remove the excess cardboard with a utility knife (fig. 1).

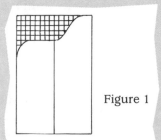

Figure 1

2. Cut fabric at least 2 inches larger than the screen around all sides (fig. 2).

3. Spray the front of the board with adhesive spray. (Allow the adhesive to dry until it's tacky.) Place the fabric (right side up) directly on top of the cardboard and smooth it out carefully.

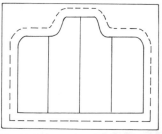

Figure 2

4. Turn the board over and bring the edges of the fabric to the wrong side of the board. You may need to clip notches in the fabric so it will fold smoothly over the edges (especially if they are curved). Secure the folded fabric on the wrong side with fabric glue or adhesive (fig. 3).

5. Finish the back with a complementary fabric. You can add trim to the front to accent the shaped edge.

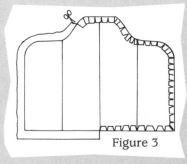

Figure 3

choice. Add a decal to each knob (available in craft stores) to carry out a decorative theme.

※ Another way to make a table is to create a base from a length of picket fence. Trim off the bottom of the pickets to table height. Make a square from four separate pieces of fence and secure it together with angle brackets. Place a round piece of glass on top of the picket fence base.

※ Transform an unfinished cabinet or armoire into your favorite piece of furniture by replacing its glass panes with wire mesh. Add decorative upholstery tacks in a pleasing pattern on the front of the piece and you're done!

※ Slipcovers are a cost-effective way to bring new life to aged and worn furniture. Slipcovers can be professionally made, but many linen and home-furnishing stores carry a line of ready-made slip-covers. Don't discount the idea of making a slipcover yourself, as many styles are easy to make. Select a closely woven fabric that is wide enough to minimize the need for seaming. The fabric should also be preshrunk to avoid any unhappy surprises when the slipcovers are cleaned. Trims like braid, fringe, and cording are the perfect accents for slipcovers. Select trims that are preshrunk and colorfast, unless you plan to dry clean the slipcovers.

※ Other quick furniture cover-ups could include a bed sheet, a quilt, or even a tablecloth draped casually over the entire piece and tucked into the crevices to define the shape and hold the cover in place.

※ When reupholstering furniture, always select the best quality of fabric you can afford. Firmly woven heavy fabrics are the most durable.

※ Give dated and ugly wooden furniture a face-lift by adding decorative pine-plank paneling and molding to each drawer front. To begin, remove any existing hard-ware and sand off most of the existing finish. Attach the molding to the outside edge of the drawer fronts with wood glue and finishing nails. Cut the pine-plank paneling so it fits exactly inside the molding frame; attach it with wood glue and finishing nails. Paint the entire unit as desired. Finally, drill holes for new hardware.

☀ Turn an out-of-style upholstered chair into an eye-catcher by painting the entire chair—cushions and all! Use specially formulated fabric paints that are soft to the touch and create whimsical or realistic designs. Paint any exposed wood (such as the legs) to go with the newly created fabric design.

☀ Make a tabletop from felt-covered plywood to enlarge the size of a small dining room table. Test the size of the piece of plywood for stability on your table before you cover it with felt. You can even do as my friend Andrea did and use this tip to cover a pool table so you can use it to eat on between games.

Hints for Buying Quality Secondhand Furniture

Is that $30 sofa really a good deal? Do you need help at yard sales deciding what's a treasure and what's junk? Here are some tips.

☀ Turn furniture shopping into an adventure. Be a regular at flea markets and shop at yard sales religiously (go first thing in the morning for the best selection). Make friends with the staff at your local secondhand store to find out when new merchandise arrives. Be there when they take the new items off the truck!

☀ When deciding on a furniture piece, have a plan in mind before you buy. Furniture should be practical to your lifestyle. Do you have children and pets? Then you may want to consider easy-to-clean wood finishes that won't show every fingerprint. Consider which furniture pieces can do "double duty." For example, can you use a coffee table for casual dining? If there is a possibility that you will be moving in the near future, consider whether the piece you are looking at will adapt easily to a new room arrangement.

❋ Draw a rough floor plan and even take a photograph of the room so that you can easily visualize pieces of furniture you find. Also keep handy measurements of spaces where you are considering placing a piece of furniture.

❋ Select furniture pieces that can be used interchangeably. For example, a chair used in the dining room can be pulled into the living room if needed, and a chair from the living room can be used in the dining room.

❋ Details make the difference. Look for great lines and interesting features in furniture that will be even more exciting when painted. For example, carvings add a lot of interest to the finished piece.

❋ Test each piece of furniture to see if it wobbles; avoid it if it does unless it only needs loose screws or pegs tightened.

❋ Joints, where two parts of a wooden piece of furniture meet, should be tight and smoothly matched.

❋ Drawers should be assembled with dovetail joints, not nails. They should glide smoothly and have automatic stops. Cabinet drawers should fit flush when closed.

❋ The finish should be smooth on all sides of the furniture piece—not just the top surface. Check the legs as well for any rough spots.

❋ Hardware should be screwed, not nailed, to doors and drawers.

❋ Avoid buying old and used furniture pieces that have missing wooden parts, pieces that are cracked, or pieces that show obvious signs of repair efforts attempted by the previous owner.

❋ Not all pieces of old furniture need refinishing. Many just need a little care and cleaning. To test whether the piece you have needs refinishing or cleaning, rub the dirtiest spot you can find on the piece with a good-quality

WHAT SHOULD I LOOK FOR IN FURNITURE?

furniture cleaner. If the spot comes clean and you can see the woodgrain clearly, you don't have to refinish the piece.

❋ These are the three best shapes to look for when buying used sofas and chairs: a camelback sofa, which lends itself to all decors; an overstuffed sofa with loose cushions, which can be recovered easily by draping fabric over the sides, back, and front, and covering individual cushions in coordinating fabrics; and a wing chair, which is a classic shape that always looks great.

A Repair to Remember

Rescued furniture may need tender loving repairs before it can withstand the abuse of everyday use. Here are some pointers for furniture repair.

❋ Resecure dovetail joints that have become loosened over the years with wood glue and clamps.

❋ Pound pegs back into their holes with a wood mallet or a hammer and block of wood (to protect the finish). Pound gently to avoid further destruction.

❋ Depending on the finish you want, you may choose to leave the dents and cracks as they are—they add character to the piece. However, if you want to remove these imperfections, fill them with wood putty, let them dry, and then sand them smooth. Wipe away any residue with a tack cloth.

❋ To repair a loose chair rung, remove the rung and scrape off the dried glue. (Don't forget to scrape out the hole.) If the end of the rung is too small to fit securely in the hole, wrap the rung end with cheesecloth that has been saturated in glue. Allow to dry. Test-fit the rung and sand off the glued ends if needed. Apply fresh glue, turn the chair upside down, and slip the rung into place. Tie a rope around the chair legs to hold the rungs tight.

Add Punch with Paint

Inexpensive, colorful, and creative finishes can be applied to most wood pieces. Before beginning, the previous finish has to be removed. Consult a paint professional for the best method for your furniture. Usually, a latex primer is all you need to cover previously painted surfaces. Protect your newly painted furniture with two to three coats of clear polyurethane; allow the surface to dry between coats.

☼ Don't worry about rules or mistakes when painting furniture. Remember to have fun.

☼ Before beginning a painting project, rub your hands with baby oil to make it easier to remove the paint from your hands afterwards.

☼ Combine stained and painted wood on the same furniture piece. For example, stain the surface of a coffee table a warm color (such as pecan), and paint the base and legs a strong decorator color that coordinates well with the stain.

I HAVE A GREAT PIECE OF FURNITURE. HOW CAN I TURN IT INTO A MASTERPIECE?

☼ For a touch of whimsy, paint a flea-market chest to look as if pieces of clothing are coming out of the drawers.

☼ Try some good, old-fashioned finger-painting for your next project. Use the paint of your choice and draw grids, flowers, and geometric designs onto the surface with just a touch of hand. (Find out more about this technique on page 203.)

☼ Create one-of-a-kind plaid furniture with a roller that has been specially sculpted in various widths. (See page 193 for complete instructions.)

☼ Repaint wicker furniture to give it a new lease on life. If you're adventurous, add stripes. To begin, paint the entire chair with white latex paint. Measure the piece and determine how many and how wide to paint the stripes. Hint: An uneven number of stripes looks the best. Center one stripe directly in the middle of the chair for balance. Using painter's masking tape, mark off the stripes. Using a 1-inch paintbrush, paint the edges of each stripe with your selected color. Fill in the center portion of the stripe with a foam brush. Allow the paint to dry before you remove the tape.

☼ Another technique that looks great on wicker is to paint a piece of wicker furniture with a dark basecoat. When almost dry, "age" the wicker by removing paint from the areas that receive the most wear and abrasion (seat, back, arms) with steel wool. Allow the chair to dry completely before adding a second and lighter color. Use steel wool to remove this second coat in the same abrasion areas. Allow the second coat to dry completely before painting the entire piece with wood stain (wipe off the excess stain before it dries).

☀ Revive an old, worn, metal daybed or headboard with metallic paint. After applying a suitable primer and

Fast Furniture Fix-Ups

Great wooden furniture finds may come with some surface and odor problems that can easily be corrected. Refer to the list below for easy solutions.

Musty Smell

- Stick cloves in a green apple and place it in a drawer or other area that needs refreshing.
- Mix 2 teaspoons of Australian tea tree oil (available in health food stores) and 2 cups of water. Spray the inside of drawers with this mixture.

Scratches

- Use shoe polish, crayon, or felt-tipped marker to color in scratches. Select colors that match or blend with the furniture finish. Tan or natural colors work with light wood; cordovan or reddish-brown colors work well on cherry wood.
- Sometimes a dampened tea bag will cover a scratch. Also try a broken walnut or a pecan meat. Rub the tea bag or nut meat over the scratch or nick until it is no longer visible. Clean and buff the area with a clean cloth.

White Rings and Water Marks

- Apply a paste made from salt and mineral oil directly over the mark. Rub gently in the direction of the woodgrain. Wipe the spot dry immediately with a clean cloth, and apply wax or polish.
- Wipe the ring first with a cloth dipped in lighter fluid and then with a mixture of rottenstone (a polishing material available in hardware stores)

allowing time for it to completely dry, spray the entire bed frame with a dull metallic spraypaint. Mask off areas you want to remain this finish with masking tape and/or newspaper, then spray remaining sections with a flat black paint. Highlight these black-painted features by spattering an acrylic metallic paint on the area. For more definition, apply the same paint to any crevices with a small brush. Spray the entire painted surface with a satin acrylic sealer.

and salad oil. Wipe the spot dry immediately with a clean cloth, and apply wax or polish.

White Marks

- Squeeze nongel white toothpaste onto a damp cloth and buff the area. For a tough stain, mix toothpaste and baking soda and apply. Clean surface with an oil soap (such as Murphy's Oil Soap).

- Rub the stain with vegetable oil or mayonnaise. Wipe it dry and apply wax or polish.

Alcohol Stains

- Mix a paste of linseed oil and rottenstone. Then rub the paste onto the stain, rubbing with the grain of the wood. Wipe the area dry immediately with a clean cloth, and apply wax or polish.

Cigarette Burns

- Rub the area with a paste made from fine fireplace ash and lemon juice.

Chewing Gum or Wax

- Harden the wax or gum with an ice cube. (Wrap the ice cube in cloth to avoid more damage.) Carefully scrape away the substance; reharden it as necessary while you work. Wipe the cleaned area with a cloth dipped in mineral spirits; buff with a soft, dry cloth.

Paint Marks

- For fresh marks, remove latex paint with water and an oil-base paint with mineral spirits or fine steel wool dipped in paste wax. If the marks have been there for a while, soak the spot with linseed oil until the paint softens, and carefully scrape it off with a putty knife. Remove any remaining residue with a paste of linseed oil and rottenstone. Wipe dry and wax.

Special Techniques

You can get as creative as you want when decorating furniture. Review these ideas before beginning your project. The techniques are easy to do and the results are spectacular. If you are really ambitious, combine two or more techniques on the same project.

Spatter Paint: Paint furniture in the color of your choice. Then using a toothbrush and as many different colors as you wish, dip the brush into paint (one color at a time) and run your fingers over the bristles to spatter paint over the furniture surface. You may want to thin the spatter paint slightly with water.

Dye: Consider dyeing wooden pieces of furniture instead of painting or staining. Dyeing lets the grain of the wood show through. This technique also works well on wicker or straw. Select a fabric dye in the color of your choice. Mix the dye with water as directed on the package. Use a foam paintbrush or soft rag to cover all the surfaces with dye. Smaller items can be submerged into a dye bath. Allow the piece to dry thoroughly. Option: Decorate the surface with stencils. Simply mix up another batch of dye in a contrasting color. Using a foam brush, stencil designs where desired. Allow them to dry. Spray the finished project with sealer or apply a coat of polyurethane. (See page 201 for more about this technique.)

Painting: Paint the surface of the furniture in a color of your choice. Add decorative shapes with acrylic paint. Add dots, swirls, dashes, or geometric designs for color and interest. For clean-line stripes and geometrics, use low-tack painter's masking tape to mark guidelines. For unusual designs, "paint" with kitchen tools such as mashers or vegetable rufflers, the ends of clothespins, or a metal ruler edge. Or try painting each area a different color for a patchwork look. Add simple motifs to make the areas look like different prints of fabric.

Decals: Self-adhesive decals are widely available in craft stores. These decals are usually "picture perfect" and give a realistic hand-painted look. Apply decals over a freshly painted surface that has been allowed to dry thoroughly.

Wallpaper: You probably think covering furniture with wallpaper is going too far. But just think of the possibilities (a chest of drawers, a coffee table, a bookshelf). Prepare the furniture pieces by sanding all rough edges and wiping away dust with a damp cloth. Prime the entire surface with primer and allow it to dry. Determine which areas of the piece will be wallpapered and which will be painted. Mask the areas that are not to be painted using painter's low-tack tape. Paint the rest of the piece in the color of your choice. Prepare the areas to be papered with wallpaper sizing. Cut the wallpaper to fit. Follow the manufacturer's instructions for immersing prepasted wallpaper in water or apply paste to the wallpaper. Apply the paper to the surface; smooth out any air bubbles with a wallpaper brush and remove any excess adhesive with a damp sponge. To secure the edges, roll them with a seam roller (apply firm, even pressure); be careful not to squeeze out the glue. Allow the entire project to dry and then apply two coats of polyurethane. Let the piece dry thoroughly between coats.

Fabric: Cover the drawer fronts of bureaus or chests with leftover fabric. Cut paper patterns to fit each area to be covered by tracing each drawer front. Cut fabric the same size as the pattern. Spray the wrong side of the fabric pieces with adhesive and place them on the areas to be covered. Hint: Allover fabric prints are the easiest to work with as they don't require matching. For added protection, apply a coat of polyure-thane to fabric-covered surfaces.

Decoupage: This finishing technique can be as simple or elaborate as you want. The basic process of decoupage is to apply cut paper to a surface with slightly thinned white glue. The surface is then sealed with several coats of polyurethane or a special decoupage coating (available in craft stores). Use images from wallpaper, greeting cards, book illustrations, calendars, or maps. Consider using this technique on table surfaces, folding screens, and bookcases.

Gel Stain Marquetry: You don't have to be proficient in carpentry to try this technique. In fact, the look of inlaid wood is created entirely by gel stains. The marquetry design can be as simple or as complex as you desire. Begin with an unfinished piece of furniture that has been lightly sanded until smooth. Remove all dust particles from the surface. Brush a prestain wood conditioner on the entire surface. Create your own

Continued

design on a piece of paper. Transfer the design onto the wood. Decide on color placement and mark off all the same-colored sections with painter's tape. Fill the sections with a gel stain. Remove the tape and allow the stain to dry. Stain the remaining sections in the same manner with a different color of stain. When all sections are stained, outline them with a black opaque marker. Seal the entire piece with a coat of varnish (not water-based).

Combing: Combed designs are applied over a freshly painted surface in a contrasting color. Special combing tools are available to create different effects, but you can use a regular hair comb, a notched piece of balsa wood, or a piece of sturdy cardboard wrapped with rubber bands. Before beginning, experiment on a scrap of wood or cardboard. Try dragging the comb in a straight line, making curly lines, or even making circles. If you make a mistake, simply paint over the area with the base color and start over. Apply several coats of acrylic sealer or interior polyurethane when the piece is completely painted and thoroughly dry.

Upholstering: Fabric and batting are the main ingredients used when upholstering the top of a side table, nightstand, vanity table, sewing table, coffee table or even a dresser with pedestal or inset legs. This finishing technique adds softness to otherwise harsh furniture lines. Cut the fabric and batting larger than the surface to be covered. Measure the length and width of the table; then add its thickness, the width of the turn under plus 1 inch to all sides.

Center the batting over the tabletop and staple the edges to the under-side of the table. The batting layer should be firm and taut with neat corners. Repeat the process with lightweight clear vinyl for a moisture barrier. Finally, center the fabric over the table. Begin at the center of one side. Pull the fabric snug and secure it temporarily with a pushpin to the underside of table. Repeat this step directly opposite the starting point. Repeat with both ends of the table. Staple the fabric smoothly around the perimeter of the table. Note: For extra stability, you may want to wrap the cut edge of the fabric around upholsterer's tape (available at fabric stores) and staple through all the layers. Spray the entire surface with a protective coating specially formulated for fabrics.

6 Floors, Stairs, and Doors

How you treat floors, stairs, and doors can make a strong design statement in your house. A little creativity goes a long way when you focus your decorating efforts on these often-forgotten areas.

On the Floor Front

The expansive area underfoot is literally and figuratively a foundation for your decorating scheme. How you treat this area has great impact on the room.

☼ Paint, stamp, or stencil a hardwood floor with a border or an overall design. Select a geometric design or a more detailed motif. Always protect your painted surface with several layers of clear varnish or polyurethane.

☼ In lieu of carpet in a nursery or child's room, paint the floor a color that goes with the room's color scheme. Paint some geometric shapes in many colors and add some numbers and maybe even the alphabet so the floor can double as a learning tool.

☼ Terra cotta tiled floor is often an expensive feature of the home. However, you can create the look of a terra cotta floor with a little paint and a stamp for a fraction of the cost. (See page 198 for complete instructions.)

☼ Liven up oak flooring by installing black electrician's tape in a geometric shape directly onto the floor. This is perfect for apartment dwellers. Just pull up the tape when you move.

☀ For a whimsical floor covering, paint a trompe l'oeil (which is French for "fool the eye") area rug complete with fringe and all the colorful details you would find in a purchased rug. Look in decorating catalogs for inspiration for your rug design.

☀ A worn pine floor is a perfect candidate for painted designs. Straight-line borders or geometric designs are great choices. Latex paint, protected by coats of clear varnish or polyurethane, is the usual choice for this type of project.

Tread on Me

What you put on a floor can pull a room together instantly. However, your creativity doesn't have to lie dormant when treating this important area of the room.

☀ Install as plush a carpet as your budget allows for a feeling of luxury. The addition of carpet padding will contribute greatly to a luxurious feeling.

☀ If you have wall-to-wall carpeting that you cannot re-place, consider adding an area rug in a strategic place and build a conversation area or dining space around it.

☀ An alternative to wall-to-wall carpeting is several area rugs in the same room. Rugs not only add color and texture, but they can "anchor" a seating area, lead the eye down a hall, and define and separate spaces.

☀ Perk up an otherwise plain kitchen rug by poking holes around the perimeter of a ready-made wedge-shaped rug with an ice pick. Use a crochet hook to pull weaving loops (the kind children use to make potholders) through each hole and secure by pulling one end through the other. Use as many colors as desired. If you want, add some polka dots or stamped designs to the center area of the rug with matching acrylic paints.

MY FLOORS ARE BARE AND UGLY. WHAT CAN I DO THAT DOESN'T COST A FORTUNE?

☼ Colorful area rugs sprinkled around the room can make an otherwise dull carpet come alive (or hide worn spots).

☼ An artistic alternative to an area rug is a hand-painted floorcloth. Use artist's canvas (available in art supply stores) and any leftover paint you may have from painting the walls to paint the design of your choice. Use this floorcloth as you would an area rug. Don't forget to coat the completed cloth with polyurethane to protect your masterpiece. (See page 192 for complete details on this project.)

Determining Area Rug Sizes

The size of an area rug is determined mainly by how the furniture is arranged and the natural traffic patterns within a room. Here are some guidelines for choosing the right size rug for any room.

• Ideally, the first step you take into a room should be onto the flooring. Your subsequent steps should be onto the area rug.

• If furniture in a living room is arranged near the center of the room, all legs of the furniture should be on the area rug. If furniture is arranged around the perimeter of the room, the front legs of the furniture pieces should be placed far enough onto the rug that they won't slip off.

• Ideally, in a dining room, all chair and table legs should be on the area rug even when a chair is pulled away from the table.

6: – Floors, Stairs, and Doors

☼ Paint a freehand design or use precut stencils to decorate
a sisal rug.

Upstairs, Downstairs

Staircases are often an area of a home that is neglected or
under-decorated. The diagonal lines of a staircase are an
ideal area to add your personal touch.

☼ Instead of carpeting a staircase, decorate
the stairs with paint, stain, tile, wallpaper, or a combination of any of
the above. Stain or paint the
treads in one color and add
a patterned design on
each riser (the vertical
part of each step).

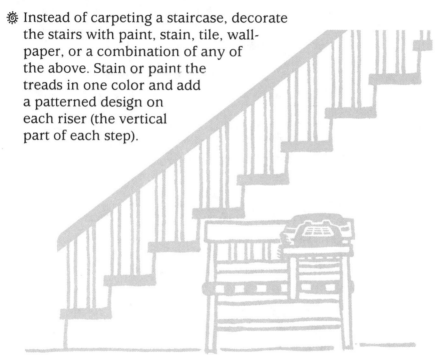

☼ The unused area below the stairway is a good place for a
special piece of furniture.

☼ Consider the wall next to the stairway as a potential
portrait gallery. Hang pictures that include family members. Don't forget your long-lost ancestors and your
beloved pets.

☼ Decorate your banister seasonally. Entwine garlands of
greenery, autumn leaves, silk flowers, tulle, and even
shiny white lights.

☼ Display baskets, stuffed animals, dolls, or even a pottery
collection on the steps.

☀ Stencil a wandering ivy or floral design climbing the stairs. Continue the design as the surface changes from drywall to wood floor to carpet.

Doors to Success

Look at doors as the gateway to your world. Don't ignore this opportunity to greet your guests in style.

☀ Decorate French doors as if they were windows. That is, select an actual window treatment to go above and beside the doors. Make sure the design you select will not interfere with the movement of the doors.

☀ For an ultimate surprise, leave the French doors undressed—but paint a trompe l'oeil "curtain" around them. Keep the other walls plain so as not to distract from this new focal point.

☀ Cover door panels with wallpaper that matches the walls in the room. Trim the outside edges of the wallpaper panels with decorative molding.

☀ Drape grapevines over the doorway. Add artificial grapes, ribbons, corks, raffia, bows, or seasonal decorations.

☀ Paint each door in a long hallway a different color. Select colors of the same intensity or strength.

☀ Cover a bedroom or bathroom door with postcards you have collected either from friends traveling or your own getaways and glue them to the surface of a door. Once the postcards are in place, coat the entire door with shellac.

☀ Decorate a sewing room door with logos cut from various fabric store bags acquired during your travels. Coat the door with polyurethane.

☀ On the door into the laundry area, hang a length of rope to simulate a clothesline. Use miniature clothespins to hang doll clothes from the rope.

☀ Fill the raised or recessed areas of your bedroom closet door with designs and/or motifs cut from wallpaper borders. Using small, pointed, paper scissors, cut around

6 – Floors, Stairs, and Doors

the outline of the selected motifs. Wallpaper borders provide a continuous design that fills the vertical area of doors.

❂ Surprise your summer guests by cross-stitching flowers or other summertime motifs onto the screen in your screen door. You may need to use all six threads in a strand of embroidery floss to fill the holes in the screen.

❂ Paper an entire door with pages from old books, your favorite sheet music, or articles cut from the newspaper. Glue the paper to the door with wallpaper paste. You can apply a varnish to protect the paper from dirt. You may want to "frame" the outside edges of the door with colorful grosgrain ribbon.

❂ Make a chalkboard door by applying several coats of chalkboard paint directly to the door front. Trim the outer edges of the door in a semi-gloss or high-gloss latex paint for easy cleaning.

❂ Supply colorful paint to ambitious youngsters and have them paint the door to their room with their hands. Simply dip their hands in paint and press them to the surface of the door.

7 Garden Variety

If you can only have one accessory to decorate your home, select a handful of fresh flowers. They can be picked from your own garden or purchased. Place them everywhere—in a bathroom, in an unused fireplace opening, and in buckets or other colorful containers at each doorway.

Containing Information

Flower containers can be as elegant as a crystal vase or as everyday as a tin can. Let the flowers—not the container—dominate the arrangement.

❀ Flower lovers can never have too many glass jars or interesting bottles. Whatever they originally held, they are perfect receptacles for fresh-cut flowers.

❀ More inexpensive, yet creative, container ideas include decorated pitchers, teacups, oil-and-vinegar bottles, old crocks, interesting hats (place a bowl or round vase in the opening), or even paper bags!

❀ Use old water pitchers, antique teapots, or chipped and tattered terra cotta pots as casual containers for an impromptu flower arrangement.

❀ Create a centerpiece with several miniature vases filled with a variety of flowers and group them together on a tray or mirror.

☀ Take advantage of natural containers: scoop out a hole in a squash or pumpkin to create a perfect fall vase, or use scooped-out lemons in the spring and summer months. Place a glass or plastic container in the opening to hold the flowers. You may need to add a piece of florist foam inside the container. If you are using a large pumpkin, slice off the top as if making a jack-o-lantern. After the "insides" have been removed, replace the top of the pumpkin and pierce holes in the top (an apple corer or awl works well for this). Then insert the flower stems through the holes and into the florist foam.

☀ Don't discard broken flower heads. Float several blooms in a favorite crystal bowl. Add a floating candle or two for a glowing effect. Or place single blooms in champagne glasses and set one at each place setting at a dinner party.

☀ Turn plain clay flowerpots into works of art with simple painted designs. Add your favorite plants. (See page 208 for ideas.)

☀ Use a discarded suitcase or train case as a container in which to display your plants. The suitcase may be deep enough to hide any existing containers that fill the open areas.

☀ Suspend an old glass lampshade upside down from chains secured to a plant hanger in the ceiling and fill it with cascading plants such as ivy.

Flower Power

Flowers from your garden are very special. Display them with care. Here are some tips to make them look their best.

☀ Pick flowers in the early morning or in the evening to keep them from wilting.

☀ After you have gathered the flowers, cut the stems to assorted lengths. Use at least three different kinds of flowers in one arrangement (unless, of course, it is a simple bouquet of daisies, tulips, or other similar flower). Use flowers from various stages of development—include some buds and partly opened flowers—so the bouquet will last.

I LOVE FRESH FLOWERS. WHAT KIND OF CONTAINER SHOULD I USE TO DISPLAY THEM?

Self-Containment

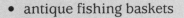

Use your imagination when looking for plant containers. Almost anything can be used as a planter. Here are some suggestions to start you on your way.

- antique fishing baskets
- antique or antique-looking milk cans
- birdcages
- claw-foot porcelain bathtubs
- feeding troughs
- galvanized steel buckets
- large tin cans
- wheelbarrows, new or old
- milk pails
- old flower carts
- old garden boots
- weathered watering cans
- wooden toolboxes

☼ If a stem breaks, insert it into a clear drinking straw and then place it in the vase.

☼ Place the tallest flower in the center of the container and arrange smaller flowers so they appear to be radiating from it.

☼ When flowers in a large arrangement begin to droop, remove the tired and dried flowers; use the remaining flowers in several smaller arrangements and distribute them throughout the house.

Plant Stand

If you have a green thumb when it comes to growing plants, what can you do with the fruits of your labor?

☼ Use an old stepladder to display potted plants. Don't forget to hang baskets of plants from the ladder's side supports.

❀ Transform a plain, ordinary terra cotta urn into an expensive-looking verdigris pot. (See page 208 for instructions for this technique.)

❀ Stack some books to make a stand for a beautiful or unusual plant.

❀ Convert a birdcage into a planter. This container can be placed on a table or suspended from the ceiling. It's perfect for ivy!

I HAVE A GREEN THUMB. HOW CAN I DISPLAY MY FLOWERS AND PLANTS CREATIVELY?

❀ An ordinary plastic nursery pot can be transformed into an attractive container for your plants. Use a glue gun to cover the outside of the container with moss (available at craft stores). Then glue strips of bark (also available at craft stores) around the rim. To keep the moss looking fresh, mix together the following ingredients in a spray bottle: 3 drops of green food coloring, 1 drop of yellow food coloring, and 1 1/2 cups of water. Lightly mist the moss.

❀ Use an outdoor trellis indoors to create vertical interest in an otherwise plain corner or to cover up a less-than-perfect wall. Attach lots of climbing plants and baskets of flowers to the trellis slats. Position the trellis near the window to make sure the plants have enough light.

❀ Tuck a few silk flowers into a green plant for a colorful surprise.

❀ Don't pack away your white Christmas lights—adorn the branches of a large house plant or tree year round.

Natural Wonders

Flowers are not the only objects from the great outdoors that make interesting arrangements.

❀ Individual bowls of pine cones, leaves, nuts, or gourds placed around the house elegantly announce the arrival of fall.

❀ Boughs of holly add hearty color to rooms throughout the winter—not just in December.

❀ Layer a variety of dried seeds in a brandy snifter for a natural display of color.

Window Gardens

City dwellers have known about window gardens for years. Now it's time for the rest of the world to discover and enjoy them.

☀ Create an indoor window garden using miniature fruit plants. Dwarf varieties of citrus fruits (such as lemons and oranges) are good choices for colorful window gardens.

☀ Create an herb box for the kitchen. Good cooking herbs include dill, parsley, rosemary, basil, oregano, marjoram, and dill. You can also use the herbs from this garden to make flavored vinegars and oils.

☀ Plant a pot of miniature roses for a living- or dining-room accent.

☀ A collection of cacti is perfect for a sunny den, kitchen, or garden room.

Budding Decorators

You've spent a lot of time selecting the perfect furniture, rugs, and accessories that reflect your decorating style, but don't stop there. Why not create flower arrangements to complement your decor? Here are some floral ideas to suit your home.

Traditional

Arrange a mixture of flowers (roses, gladiola, irises, carnations, and lilies) in a crystal, glass, silver, or porcelain container.

Contemporary

This style of decorating requires dramatic flower choices like anthuriums, heliconia, and orchids. Place them in a frosted glass or metallic-finish vase.

A Rosy Outlook

The rose motif is used in many decorating schemes and is always a favorite accent. You can enjoy fresh roses in your home year round. To keep your roses looking fresh longer, follow these hints.

※ If you are using a backyard rosebush for your bouquets, cut fresh roses in the early morning but wait until after the dew has dried.

※ Put cut roses in fresh water immediately after picking. If possible, bring a bucket of water with you to the garden to hold the freshly cut roses.

※ Recut the tips of the stems at an angle before arranging the roses in a vase. Cut the tips under warm water to prevent the formation of tiny air pockets that block the

Casual

A piece of pottery or an informal glass pitcher is the perfect receptacle for sunflowers, daisies, or hydrangea.

Victorian

Pale fragrant flowers such as roses and peonies are reminiscent of this era. Place them in clear glass, silver, or crystal containers.

American Country

Woven baskets filled with mixed spring flowers like yarrow, wild roses, scabiosa, and heather are perfect for this decor choice. Also perfect are blooming plants, herbs, wreaths, and swags.

ends of the stems and keep them from absorbing water. Let the freshly cut stems soak 30 minutes before arranging the flowers.

※ Remove any leaves or thorns that will be submerged in the water. If not removed, these parts of the stem will rot, producing bacteria that will shorten the life of the roses.

※ Roses drink a lot of water so change the water every day.

※ Every time you change the water, recut the stems.

※ The easiest way to arrange a dozen roses is to arrange florist tape (available in floral departments in craft stores) in a grid pattern over the opening of a vase. Place the stems of the roses in individual openings. Start with the tallest stem in the exact center. Then surround that rose with the remaining flowers. The secret of this arrangement is to crisscross the stems in the water so the roses billow from the container.

Dried Flowers

Drying extends the life of real flowers indefinitely. You'll get years of enjoyment from one simple bouquet if you use dried flowers.

※ Hang an assortment of dried flowers as a valance over a kitchen window instead of a traditional fabric valance. For seasonal changes, tie small bouquets of dried flowers in ribbons that reflect the time of the year.

※ Make potpourri with broken or less-than-perfect dried flowers.

※ Make a topiary so you can enjoy your garden throughout the year. Gather assorted dried plant material and arrange it around a moss-covered Styrofoam ball. Add color by inserting seasonal fruit (such as grapes, lemons, apples, and oranges that have been secured to a florist's pick with wire or glue). To stabilize the topiary, insert one end of a tree branch into the Styrofoam ball and place the opposite end in a heavy container (such as a clay pot) that has been filled with stones or dirt.

Drying Flowers

To air-dry flowers, follow these simple steps:

1. Pick plants at all stages of their blooming cycle; some flowers dry best when picked as buds, while others work best if their blooms are completely open.

2. Pick the flowers in the late afternoon after all traces of moisture in the air are gone (rain, dew, fog, and so on). Avoid picking flowers during extreme heat so they won't droop.

3. Remove the leaves from the stems and tie the flowers into small bunches (no more than 6 flowers to a bunch).

4. Hang the bunches upside down from a wire or cord in a dark, dry, warm place for a week or so (colors have a tendency to fade if they are exposed to sunlight when drying). Check the flowers every 3 days or so to prevent overdrying.

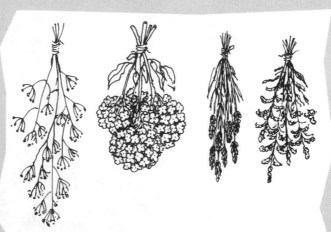

5. Always dry more flowers than you think you'll need (dried flowers break easily).

Great Flowers for Dry Arrangements

Here are the most common and popular "ingredients" for dry floral arrangements (including wreaths) are

Ammi majus

anise hyssop

artemisia

baby's breath

bachelor's button

celosia

dwarf goldenrod

echinacea purpurea

feverfew

German statice

giant goldenrod

globe amaranth

heather

marigold

old rose

Queen Anne's lace

rabbit tobacco

red clover

statice

statice sinuata

strawflower

white yarrow

zinnia

Most Colorful Dry Flowers

Some flowers hold their color better than others when dried. The following is a list of flowers that dry well and retain their color best.

Silver

daisy bush

honesty

lamb's ear

melaeuca

silver king artemesia

xeranthemum

White and Cream

astilbe

baby's breath

cotton

German statice

honesty

lamb's tongue

pearly everlasting

yarrow

Purple and Blue

astilbe

bachelor's button

cornflower

delphinium

globe thistle

heather

hydrangea

lavender

statice

strawflower

teasel

Green and Brown

bamboo

bee balm

dill

hydrangea

ivy

love-in-a-mist

pin oak

Orange and Yellow

goldenrod

pot marigold

rose

santolina

statice

strawflower

tansy

yarrow

Red and Pink

astilbe

campion

celosia

globe amaranth

larkspur

rose hip

Russian statice

sunray

yarrow

Floral Traditions

Historically, flowers and herbs were said to have meanings. (See the list below for some examples.) Use this tradition to create a special bouquet, arrangement, or wreath to communicate your own special message.

amaranth – immortality

angelica – inspiration

balm – sympathy

basil – good wishes

bay – glory

bittersweet – harmony

bluebell – constancy

chervil – sincerity

chives – usefulness

clematis – mental beauty

cockscomb – affection

coriander – hidden merit

cress – stability

cumin – fidelity

dill – protection

fennel – success

fern – sincerity

holly – hope, divinity

honesty – wealth

horehound – health

ivy – God, friendship

larkspur – lightness

lavender – luck

lemon balm – comfort

lovage – gladness

marigold – uneasiness

marjoram – joy

mint – hospitality, cheer

mistletoe – love

oregano – substance

parsley – festivity

pine – humility

rose – love

rosemary – remembrance

rue – grace, clear vision

sage – wisdom

salvia, blue – I think of you

salvia, red – forever mine

sorrel – affection

spruce – stateliness

sunflower – false riches

tansy – declaration of war

tarragon – lasting interest

thyme – courage

violet – modesty

yarrow – war

8 The Great Frame-Up

A group of pictures perks up an otherwise bland wall. Keep these hints in mind when selecting, arranging, and hanging your pictures.

❀ Choose a plain wall that needs decoration for a display instead of filling every wall with pictures.

❀ Arrange the pictures on the floor first to try out different arrangements. If you have an instant camera, take pictures of arrangements you like so you won't forget them. If you don't have an instant camera, arrange the pictures on a large piece of kraft paper. Trace around the frames and then tape the entire piece of kraft paper to the wall. Use this template as a guide to install hangers.

❀ Group several sizes of pictures together. Place the largest picture in the center just below eye level and position the smaller pieces around the center.

❀ For the best visual effect, hang pictures at eye level or just below it.

❀ Hang horizontal groupings in a straight line; align the bottom edges. This arrangement will make the room look larger.

❀ Hang framed objects from a coat rack with ribbon.

❀ Use interesting doorknobs to display items such as framed pictures. Attach a doorknob to a wall, wrap a

8 – *The Great Frame-Up*

pretty ribbon around the picture's wire hanger, and tie a bow over the doorknob.

☀ Create a picture gallery on a decorative folding screen instead of on a wall.

☀ Hang various framed items from a decorative curtain rod.

☀ Set up an easel in a corner to display a favorite picture.

☀ Think "unconventional" when determining places to hang frames. For example, think of a wall book-shelf as one large surface and incorporate framed pictures into an overall arrangement of books and accessories. Hang pictures on horizontal shelves or vertical supports, or rest them against the back of the bookshelf.

☀ Install molding strips in horizontal lengths to form a ledge along one wall. Adorn these shelves with multitudes of your favorite framed photographs; lean the frames against the wall.

☀ Tie a beautiful ribbon into a bow with extra-long stream-ers and attach to the wall. Separate the streamers slightly and attach the pictures directly to the wall with the streamers draping behind the pictures.

☀ Instead of using a real ribbon, stencil a ribbon design onto a wall and arrange pictures over it as desired.

☀ Hang same-sized pictures in a vertical row from ceiling to floor.

☀ Keep in mind the proportion of a picture to nearby furniture. For example, a small picture will look lost next to or directly above a large piece of furniture.

☀ When hanging two or more pictures of the same size, space them no farther apart than the actual width of the frame.

I HAVE SO MANY PHOTOS. WHAT'S A GOOD WAY TO DISPLAY THEM AROUND THE HOUSE?

Artful Illusions

An inexpensive alternative to purchasing art is creating your own. But you don't need to be an artist. Try these suggestions when you want to fill a frame—or a wall.

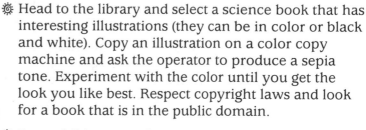

※ Head to the library and select a science book that has interesting illustrations (they can be in color or black and white). Copy an illustration on a color copy machine and ask the operator to produce a sepia tone. Experiment with the color until you get the look you like best. Respect copyright laws and look for a book that is in the public domain.

※ For a child's room, frame a page or cover of a favorite comic book for an inexpensive, yet colorful, wall decoration.

※ Frame color pictures from a favorite calendar, old sheet music, maps, postcards, greeting and note cards, or pages from a favorite fairy tale.

※ An assortment of antique or pocket watches (all set to the same time) makes an unusual display that is perfect for framing.

※ Show off antique jewelry in an aged frame.

※ Frame a map of the world.

※ Display antique kitchen utensils in a rustic or handmade frame.

※ Scour flea markets for old fruit labels that have been removed from packing crates or cans. These labels are perfect to frame and hang in the kitchen.

※ If there is a doctor in your house, frame old medicine bottles, prescriptions, or doctor's receipts for a lively conversation starter.

※ Hang interesting framed items in out-of-the-way and unexpected places. For example, hang pictures on a wall in a closet, under a bathroom sink, or on the back of a dining room chair!

※ If you don't have enough artwork to fill all the frames you have collected, why not just display the frames? Remove the backing and glass and arrange the frames attractively on a mantel. For best results, use frames of various sizes. Intersperse them with flower vases and other glass bottles for added dimension.

❁ Souvenirs from a special family vacation are worthy of framing together for years of reminiscing.

❁ For the perfect vacation souvenir, frame your vacation photos with any ticket stubs, postcards, transit tokens, receipts, or foreign currency you collected throughout your trip.

Framed!

The primary goal of framing is to choose materials that enhance the design (and don't distract from it) and preserve the artwork itself. Here are some tips for choosing the right frame.

❁ Choose simple frames for delicate artwork. Large, rough frames may be overwhelming.

❁ For pictures with warm tones, select warm wood frames. For pictures with cool tones, select a darker wood frame or a metal frame.

❁ Regular glass is more economical than nonglare glass. In addition, nonglare glass may distort the artwork—especially if it contains bright colors or fine lines.

❁ When framing a valuable or old piece of art, select an ultraviolet protective glass and acid-free paper materials such as mats and backing. Avoid hanging any artwork in direct sunlight!

❁ Mats are not only decorative—they also function to keep condensation from forming against the artwork.

❁ The color of the mat should draw attention to the picture being framed. Dark-colored mats pull the eyes into the picture; light-colored frames make the picture stand out from the wall. Dark mats should be narrower than light mats.

❁ If using multiple mats, coordinate the top mat with the picture's dominant color.

☀ Mats should be cut to measure at least twice the width of the frame.

☀ To emphasize a picture that is oriented vertically, cut the mat narrower on the sides. For a horizontal effect, do the opposite.

☀ Mats and glass are not commonly used with oil paintings.

☀ Cover a plain mat board with wallpaper fabric or wrapping paper for added style.

Ain't That a Frame?

Inexpensive or secondhand picture frames can be transformed into artful fun by following these suggestions.

☀ Embellish wood frames with an elegant gilded surface. Seal the raw wood of your frame with a wood sealer and

What's Your Hang Up?

Picture hooks, rather than nails alone are best for hanging pictures. Picture hooks distribute the weight of a picture more evenly and are less likely to pull out of the wall. Here are some guidelines.

- Adhesive hooks (white plastic squares with a hook attached) are great for lightweight items but need several hours to set before they can be used.

- Select a picture hook based on a picture's weight. The hook should support at least four times the actual weight of the picture being hung.

- For items up to 25 pounds, use drywall hangers. These easy-to-use hangers simply twist into a predrilled hole in a hollow wall.

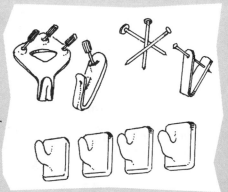

- To hang heavy objects on hollow walls, doors, and ceilings you need a drill and wall anchors or toggle bolts. A stud finder is also helpful to find the interior studs in the wall. It's best to use a stud if possible for added support when hanging a heavy object.

8 – The Great Frame-Up

allow it to dry completely. Using fine sandpaper, completely sand the frame. Paint the frame with an acrylic stain and a foam brush. After the frame is completely dry, dab on a coat of gold-colored paint. Let small areas of the stain show through. Let the frame dry; then dab on a coat of copper-colored paint over the entire surface.

❉ Completely cover the surface of a wooden frame with canceled stamps; use a tacky glue. Coat the frame with a high-gloss varnish.

❉ Cover a basic frame with an old road map. To imitate aging, paint a gel stain over the surface.

❉ Adorn a plain frame with small objects that are of personal interest. These can be charms, golf tees, buttons, party favors, even small toys such as whimsical cows.

❉ For a three-dimensional frame, nail upholstery tacks to the wooden surface. Or weave ribbon or strips of leather around frame and then add upholstery tacks where the strips connect.

❉ A terra cotta saucer can be used as a circular frame for a piece of needlework. Simply cut a piece of foam-covered frame board into a circle that fits the interior area of a saucer. Cover the board with needlework and place it inside the saucer so it fits snugly. Glue the board in place.

❉ Transform an unfinished wood frame into an interesting art piece by embellishing the front with an assortment of hinges and latches, chicken wire, seed packets, or even designs that are burned into the wood.

❉ Create a triangular-shaped frame from 2-inch-wide picture molding. Hang several triangular frames in a group for added impact.

❉ Recycle a grapevine wreath (about 8 to 10 inches in diameter) and use it as a unique frame.

9 Decorating with Fabric

Fabric adds color, pattern, and texture to a room and softens the hard edges and oddities of furniture and architectural features. This chapter will help you imagine the possibilities—and carry them out.

Pattern Play

Furniture, carpet, and paint are essential to decorating a room. But it's the prints (fabric and wallcoverings) that actually create the personality of the room.

☼ Fabrics often possess a distinct personality. For example, a tweed implies rusticity, whereas a watercolor print suggests romance and femininity.

☼ Contrary to popular belief, the style of furniture does not have to dictate the type of prints selected.

☼ Ease your eye into mixing and matching patterns by perusing wallpaper books. Traditionally, wallpaper manufacturers include several companion prints with each main wallpaper design.

☼ When mixing patterns, select fabrics and wall coverings that have colors in the same intensity. For example, if you are using dark, jewel tones for your color scheme, don't use any pastels.

9 – Decorating with Fabric

❋ To keep a room from looking too busy, introduce a
visually restful fabric in a solid color or a textured solid—
tone-on-tone fabric that is a solid color with a raised
pattern like a stripe or dot.

❋ Bring fabric swatches, or samples, home and study how
the fabric interacts with your carpet and paint selections.
Most stores that carry decorating fabrics will cut you a
swatch of fabric; some decorating stores will allow you to
check out the entire roll of fabric so you can live with
your selection for a few days. At the very least, purchase
a 1/2-yard piece of your selected fabric to refer to as you
continue to select accessories.

❋ Before making a final decision, consider how the pattern
will be viewed in its final form. For example, scrunch the
fabric together in your hand to see how it will look as a
gathered window treatment. If you have the bolt of fabric
in your home, drape the fabric over a sofa or chair to see
how the fabric will look made up in a slipcover.

❋ A good rule of thumb is to choose fabric patterns in the
same scale as what they will cover. For example, a large
fabric pattern that may look wonderful as it comes off the
roll might not be effective when it is cut up into smaller
sections because the pattern will be too chopped up.

**HOW CAN I MIX
DIFFERENT FABRICS
SUCCESSFULLY?**

❋ Select a large-scale print as the dominant pattern and use
it on the room's largest elements. For balance, repeat the
pattern on decorating pieces of descending importance.
For example, use a large print on the sofa, as a floor-
length table cover, and again as a valance.

❋ When combining several different fabrics in one room,
make sure the fabrics do not fight each other in scale and
the prints are unified through color or a recurring motif.
For example, two large floral patterns will conflict with
each other, whereas a stripe and floral in the same color
family will complement each other.

❋ Don't keep patterns in one area—mix them throughout
the room.

❋ Textured fabrics and wallcoverings can be considered a
pattern and should be used accordingly.

☀ To make a room feel larger, choose a fabric with a small motif on a light background in a dense, repetitive pattern. On the other hand, very dark colors can make a room feel cozy, small, and intimate.

☀ Use stripes and checks to bridge more complex patterns that are used in the same room. For example, if you have selected a strong print as the dominant fabric and another print as the secondary fabric, it may be too much to add a third print. This is the perfect situation to add a striped or checked fabric for visual relief.

Fabric Makeovers

Fabric is a wonderful medium for decorating. But don't plan to use fabric on just windows and pillows. Fabric lends itself well to many surfaces.

☀ If you are buying fabric for a decorating project, select fabrics made specifically for decorating and not garment fabric. Decorator fabrics are more durable for home furnishing projects and are usually 54 inches wide. Pillows, however, do not receive the wear of other home furnishings and can be made in fun, eclectic fabrics that may add whimsy to your decorating scheme. Decorator fabrics are printed so the patterns match along the selvages when sewn together; you cannot match patterns in garment fabrics without wasting big sections of fabric.

❀ When you purchase fabric, make sure you get as much fabric as you will need at the same time so you won't run the risk of having to settle for additional fabric from a different dye lot. (Different batches of dye can produce slightly different colors.)

❀ Combine fabric and lace window treatments for eclectic charm. This is an especially nice idea for kitchen, bath, and bedroom windows.

❀ Slipcovers are a cost-effective way to bring new life to aged and worn furniture. Slipcovers can be professionally made, but many linen and home-furnishing stores carry them ready-made or you can make them yourself from a commercial pattern or a how-to book. Select a wide fabric to minimize the need for seaming. The fabric should be closely woven with no reinforced "gum-backing" and preshrunk to avoid any unhappy surprises when cleaned. Trims are the perfect accent for slipcovers. Select trims that are care compatible.

❀ A worn upholstered sofa can be given an instant face-lift by drap-ing a throw or a coordinating fabric creatively over the sides or back. Also consider arranging a colorful rug over the back of a sofa and adding lots of pillows for comfort.

❀ When reupholstering furniture, always select the best quality fabric you can afford. Firmly woven heavy fabrics are most durable. Velvets and tapestries can add a special richness to a room.

☀ Other quick furniture cover-ups could include a bed sheet, a quilt, or even a colorful tablecloth.

☀ Hide architectural flaws with a beautiful quilt, shawl, or small rug displayed on the wall.

☀ Geometric or nonfloral prints—plaids, checks, dark paisleys, and stripes—are usually good fabric choices when decorating a room for a man.

☀ Sturdy fabrics such as wool, tweed, corduroy, denim, suede, and leather also add to the masculine appeal of a room.

HOW CAN I CREATE A PARTICULAR MOOD IN MY HOME?

☀ Decorating your child's room is a snap with the wide variety of children's fabrics that are available from several fabric manufacturers.

☀ Disguise uneven walls with softly gathered wall panels made from sheer or lace fabric. (See page 185 to learn how.)

☀ When decorating a nursery or a child's room, select washable fabrics instead of fabrics that require dry cleaning.

☀ Layer more than one table topper on a table for a textured and interesting look. Try different combinations. For example, combine square and round toppers or sheer and opaque fabrics.

Lacy Places

Use lace to create a romantic ambiance in every corner of your home.

☀ Combine lots of lace with yards and yards of crinkle gauze, scrim, dyed cheesecloth, or nylon netting to create a bedroom that promises to be a wonderful escape from the outside world.

☀ Lace is beautiful when used alone, but it mixes well with tatting, crochet, and eyelet or cutwork fabrics.

☀ Mix and match types of lace (an openwork panel, crocheted lace, and Battenburg lace) to create a one-of-a-kind decorative touch.

9 – Decorating with Fabric

- Lace is a very versatile fabric for decorating windows. It has a soft and open appearance, yet it is able to disguise an unattractive view and provide some privacy.

- Lacy sheer curtains are the perfect companion to both formal and informal draperies and as an undertreatment with valances.

- Lace comes in a wide variety of patterns. Coarsely woven lace works well in a kitchen, garden room, or child's room. Delicately woven lace can be used in many creative ways in bedrooms.

- Use lace to create a romantic canopy over a bed.

- Add lace motifs to simple throw pillows by handstitching them in place to the pillow front.

- Lace pillows are perfect for romantics at heart.

- Twist and twirl lengths of lace around the posts of a four-poster bed.

- For an interesting, yet inexpensive, "headboard," mount decorative hardware behind a bed and drape layers of lace (and maybe a little ribbon) for a soft and romantic look.

- Top a shelf with a lace table runner; allow the lace to drape over the front edges.

- Conceal an unattractive piece of furniture with a lace tablecloth.

- Adorn the walls with garments embellished with antique lace. Hang them on satin-covered hangers.

- Drape lengths of lace ribbon through a chandelier.

- Glue lace trims around a lampshade.

- Use lace doilies lavishly on your bedroom bureau or nightstand.

- Lace makes a wonderful dust ruffle. Select a lace with a scalloped edge and you won't have to hem it!

I'M A ROMANTIC AT HEART. HOW CAN I GET THE LOOK OF LOVE?

❀ Drape lace doilies over the edges of shelves.

❀ Glue lace trim to the edges of the shelves inside your medicine cabinet.

❀ Trim towels in the bathroom with wisps of lace and ribbon.

❀ Use a lace place mat as a romantic centerpiece on your dining room table.

❀ Glue a length of lace or a doily around the outside of a basket and fill the basket with wonderful-smelling soaps.

❀ Use a beautiful paper lace doily as a stencil and decorate a table, a bureau, a headboard, or even a bookcase. (See page 202 to learn how.)

❀ To set an elegant dinner table, always use lace-trimmed napkins.

❀ Age new lace by soaking it in tea until you get the color you desire.

❀ Use a Battenburg or other lace tablecloth as a shower curtain (don't forget to use a plastic liner).

9 – *Decorating with Fabric*

☀ Select two lace doilies and a fabric-covered pillow that is 2 to 3 inches smaller than the doilies. Place the doilies wrong sides together and stitch 1 to 1 1/2 inches from the edge. Leave an opening large enough to insert the pillow form. Handstitch the openings closed.

☀ Frame rectangles of linen with lace edging for one-of-a-kind place mats.

☀ Use pieces of lace as a stencil over fabric or ready-made items for added impact. Use lace to stencil borders on curtains and valances, on pillowcases, and on table toppers. Or create a lace-stenciled pillow. (For complete instructions turn to page 191.)

No Sewing Required

Beautiful accessories can be created without sewing a stitch. Use these ideas to make your home more cozy without using a needle and thread.

☀ Bed canopies were originally developed to ward off the chills in a drafty room but now are purely decorative in nature. A fabric canopy is simple to construct—install a

rod, plant hanger, circular toilet paper holder, or grape-vine wreath on the ceiling or wall above the bed. For best results, use 54-inch-wide fabric cut long enough to drape attractively from the hanger. To find out how long to cut the fabric, hang a string from the rod where the canopy will hang and measure the length of the string. Gather the fabric in the center and drape it over or through the hardware; hide the selvages. Hold the fabric to the sides with coordinating tiebacks.

WHAT SHOULD I USE TO CREATE A WARM, INVITING ENVIRONMENT?

❀ For a quick and easy no-sew table skirt, cut a circle of fabric 8 to 12 inches larger than needed to reach the floor. Instead of sewing a hem, simply tuck under the raw edge of the fabric along the floor.

❀ Cover a lampshade with a beautiful fabric for a complete look. Trim the top and bottom edges with decorative trim if desired. (See page 184 for complete instructions.)

❀ For an easy and beautiful window treatment, arrange a length of fabric into a tube by fusing the cut edges together. Insert a rod through the tube and hang. (See page 178 for complete instructions.)

❀ Hang a pair of folded woolen blankets together over a rod behind a bed for a wonderful, inexpensive headboard.

❀ Add a fabric canopy over an old-fashioned freestanding tub. Install a plant hanger on the ceiling in the center of the tub. Hang fabric so that it extends from the floor along one side of the tub, up through the ceiling hook, and down to the floor at the opposite side.

❀ Use leftover fabric scraps to make coordinating place mats and napkins to complement your wallpaper and window treatments. Use paper-backed fusible tape (available in fabric stores) to hem the edges of the fabric for this no-sew decorating project.

❀ Instead of painting a table, cover it with fabric. Fuse fabric to the wooden surface with a paper-backed fusible adhesive or spray the area with a glue. Add some decorative cording to the edges and a glass top (to protect the fabric), and you have a unique table that you will be proud of.

☼ – Decorating with Fabric

- ☼ Make some tiebacks for your curtains. (More information for planning and making tiebacks begins on page 179.)

- ☼ Create a colorful fabric headboard by installing a curtain rod above the bed and draping fabric over it.

- ☼ Reupholster chair cushions by wrapping a layer of batting, then fabric, around existing foam cushions as if you were wrapping a package; secure the layers in place with a few handstitches or safety pins. Batting will smooth out any irregularities and rough edges on the original cushion.

- ☼ Soften the background of a cabinet or hutch by tacking fabric to the inside back of the shelves and then covering the raw edges of the fabric with pretty trim.

- ☼ Match your pet's bed to your decor by covering a large cushion with fabric that coordinates with the room where your pet sleeps. Place the cushion in a large basket.

- ☼ Make a new pillow cover without sewing a stitch! Simply take two extra-large dinner napkins and place one on each side of an existing pillow or a purchased pillow form. Gather the corners together and wrap with a rubber band. Tie cording, ribbon, yarn, or raffia around the rubber bands.

25 Ways to Decorate with Fabric

Mix, match, and mingle fabric to your heart's content! Part of the fun in decorating is to pick pretty fabrics and think of creative ways to use them.

1. One of the easiest fabric flourishes is to include a profusion of pillows in your decorating scheme. Select your favorite fabrics and accent them with trims of all kinds.

2. Fabric accessories make an inviting dining table. Include napkins, place mats, table runners, a tablecloth, chair cushions, and cozies (padded covers) for hot dishes.

3. Cover a cigar box with fabric. It's perfect for storing your writing supplies—stamps, notecards, pen, and address book.

4. Give your bedroom a bright new look by stitching a tie-on slipcover for the headboard.

5. Cover a lampshade with a coordinating fabric—a perfect accessory for any room!

6. Don't forget to add a colorful dust ruffle to peek out from under your quilt or comforter.

7. Cover a corkboard with fabric to create a colorful wall accent and a great way to keep track of important messages.

8. Slipcover your sofa and chairs for a fresh new decorating scheme.

9. One of the most versatile furniture pieces in a home is an ottoman. Use it as extra seating, to rest your feet, or as a coffee table. Cover yours with fabric to soften its lines.

10. Cover the simple lines of several picture frames with fabric for very effective accessories.

11. Cover an otherwise unattractive table with a floor-length table skirt. Add a lavish topper for an outstanding look.

12. Add a mantel scarf to make your fireplace a colorful focal point in a room. (See page 190 for instructions.)

Continued

13. Cover your walls with fabric—either all over the room or in designated areas. Fabric-covered walls "framed" with decorative molding are an interesting way to soften a room.

14. Cover old-fashioned hatboxes with fabric and display them on shelves around the room. They'll keep important items handy while hiding the clutter.

15. Put a throw over the back of a sofa or chair or on the end of your bed.

16. For privacy, make a pull-down shade from your favorite fabric print. This idea can be used under any window treatment.

17. Make small sachets and fill them with fragrant potpourri. Tie them with a colorful ribbon and stack them together in piles of three.

18. Apply fabric decoupage to the slats and seat of an old rocking chair.

19. Cover the inside of a freestanding bookshelf with fabric that coordinates with the room.

20. Add a fabric-covered room divider or privacy screen to any room of your home. Make them in several heights for specific purposes. For example, a 3-foot-high screen can be opened in front of a nonworking fireplace. A 6-foot screen can act as a room divider for a makeshift home office. (Page 188 in chapter 19 has complete instructions for this project.)

21. A reversible table skirt is an easy way to do some quick-change decorating. Cut out two circles from different fabrics. Place the right sides of the circles together and stitch around the circumference; leave a 6-inch opening for turning. Turn the table skirt right side out and press it smooth. Handstitch the opening closed.

22. Make a body pillow that fits the entire width of the bed. Use it as a headboard when you're not sleeping.

23. Give your bathroom a fabric face-lift by stitching up a floor-length sink skirt and a coordinating shower curtain.

24. Make a reversible duvet cover for built-in decorating versatility. (Learn how on page 182.)

25. Add fabric rosettes to window treatments, pillows, or even a lampshade. (You'll find complete instructions on page 181.)

10 Fabric Furnishings

Soft accessories in magnificent fabrics are what decorating is all about. Whether you choose to make the items yourself, have them custom-made, or buy them already finished, you'll have great fun pulling everything together.

Sewing Your Decor

Sewing is a relaxing way to spend a weekend, and you'll make your house into a home when you add beautiful, handmade fabric accessories. (Even if you don't sew, you'll find ideas later in this chapter and the previous one for ways to fill your home with beautiful fabric accessories.)

❀ Home decorating patterns are offered by major pattern companies and are available in fabric stores. Take a look at the More Splash Than Cash™ decorating patterns offered through The McCall Pattern Company.

❀ Pillows are the perfect first-time project to sew. (Learn how on page 183.)

❀ For most home furnishings projects, use a 1/2-inch seam allowance unless otherwise noted.

❀ Always place pins perpendicular to the edge of the fabric; do not sew over the pins but remove them as you get to them.

❀ Backstitch at the beginning and end of each seam to secure the stitches in place.

10 – Fabric Furnishings

☼ When stitching fabric widths together for window treatments, always stitch from the bottom to the top. This way if the fabric shifts and no longer matches exactly, the mismatched area will fall in the heading area where it won't be as noticeable.

☼ Give your iron a thorough cleaning before starting any home furnishings project. Use Iron-Off Hot Iron Cleaner (available in fabric stores) to remove the residue from the iron.

☼ Use a press cloth to prevent scorch and iron shine.

Working Efficiently

To make your sewing projects go as smoothly as possible, work smart.

• Set up a permanent work area for the duration of your project. You'll lose time and momentum if you have to break down your work area after you finish each day.

• Work on as large a surface as possible. If you're using a dining room table, extend the table to its maximum size. If all else fails, move away all the furniture and use the floor.

• Make sure you have a good light source in your work area.

• Keep all of your tools orderly and within reach. Buy a good pair of scissors for your sewing projects—do not cut paper with this pair because paper will dull the blades and make cutting your fabric too difficult.

• When sewing large volumes of fabric, keep the weight of the fabric from pulling on the needle by positioning a chair in front of and behind the sewing machine to "catch" the fabric as you sew.

• Wind three bobbins before you start a large project; you will always have a spare at your fingertips.

• Start each project with a new needle; needles become dull through use. Select a needle that is compatible with the weight of your

❁ To achieve crisp edges when pressing a lined project, first press the seam open. Then arrange the project so that the lining and decorator fabrics are equally lined up and neither shows on the opposite side. Press again if necessary.

❁ Press by lifting the iron up and down. "Sweeping" the iron back and forth stretches the bias edges and seams.

❁ Always work with clean hands during the construction process. Avoid eating and drinking in your work area because spills and stains can be the downfall of any sewing project.

fabric. (The needle package usually provides you with this information.) Needles break, so always have extras on hand.

• Keep a clean trash can near your work area to throw away scraps and loose threads as you sew.

• Tidy up at the end of each workday; it's easier to get going the next day with everything in its place.

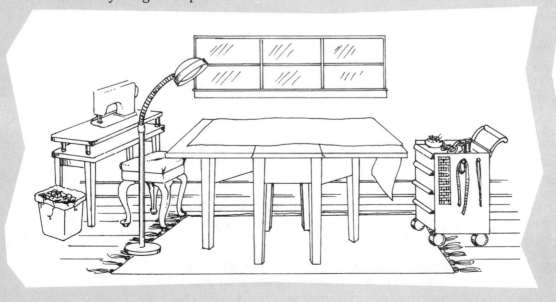

☼ In theory, fabric needs to be exactly "on grain," or straight, for home furnishings projects to be perfect. But few fabrics are printed precisely on grain. Take a few extra minutes to make sure your fabric is ready to be cut. (Learn how to straighten fabric on page 174.)

☼ To make your home furnishings project look more professional, match the repeats at all the seams so the joined fabric widths give the illusion of one large piece of fabric. Patterned fabrics have motifs or designs that repeat uniformly. A "repeat" is the length of one full motif, the distance from an element on the motif to the same element on the next motif. The easiest way to match the motifs exactly is to "fuse baste" the seams by using a paper-backed fusible tape. (For complete instructions, turn to page 175.)

Fringe Binge

Fringe and trims are the perfect accent for many items in your home. Use them to update tired or old furniture, pillows, and accessories or to add new sparkle to a room. Here are some tips to help you use them successfully in your projects.

☼ Select trims according to the project. For example, if you are handsewing trims to an existing item (such as a pillow or ottoman) select trims that don't have a "lip" (a heading or attached seam allowance) or ones with headings that are decorative.

☼ Select trims that are in scale with the item to be embellished. For example, don't select a heavy trim for a sheer or delicate fabric. The finished project will look unbalanced.

☼ Fabric stores are not the only place to discover beautiful trims. Scour flea markets, consignment shops, and yard sales for unusual trims.

☼ Add tassels, braid, and cording to upholstered pieces, pillows, and window coverings. Don't forget to trim the smaller accents such as picture frames and bandboxes with the same trim for a coordinated look.

Trim Tricks

- Always wrap tape around cording or other trims before cutting to prevent raveling. Then cut through the taped section. Knot the cord, encase it in a seam, or glue fabric over the end to hide the tape in the finished project.

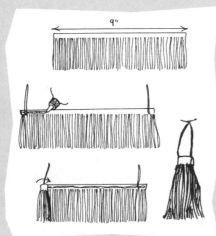

- Make your own tassels for an affordable embellishment. For each tassel, you'll need a 9-inch length of bullion fringe. To prevent the cut ends from fraying, dab them with seam sealant or wrap them with clear tape. Spread fabric glue along the top edge of the piece of fringe. At each end, pull the third or forth strand of fringe up and away from the rest of the fringe. Then roll the remaining fringe into a sausage-like shape; make sure the glue secures the top edge of the roll together. Tie the reserved two strands together in a knot for hanging the tassel.

- Wrap an old lamp base with beautiful cording. Simply glue the cording in place at the base and continue wrapping in a circular pattern until the whole base is covered. Add a new lampshade and you're done.

☀ Hang a large tassel on a drawer pull or doorknob to add color, texture, and dimension to a room.

☀ Glue braid, fringe, or trim around the top and/or bottom edge of an existing lampshade. It'll look like new!

☀ Glue lavish fringe to the arms and skirt of a wicker chair or sofa. Select a heavy fringe that won't get lost against the texture of the wicker.

☀ Glue or nail cording around the outside edge of an existing window frame. Add some fanciful bows at the corners if desired.

☀ Show off your button collection by making a square tabletopper from a neutral-colored fabric and add buttons around the perimeter. At each corner, add a decorative tassel.

Pillow Pizzazz

Pillows offer an inexpensive and colorful way to add colors, shapes, and textures to your home. Pillows soften the lines of contemporary furniture and add splashes of color where needed. Pillows are also a good way of changing decorating schemes with the seasons.

☀ Change everyday pillows to light, bright colors that remind you of the season— perhaps a lemon yellow, a fresh green, and a crisp white at the onset of spring. As fall approaches, your color choices could be gold, off-white, and sage green.

☀ To create a romantic atmosphere in any room of the house, toss together plenty of plump pillows. For a very lush effect, combine pillows made of floral needlepoint, brocades in luscious colors, and cotton moiré for sheen.

❂ Add a ruffle to soften the shape of a pillow. A ruffle can be any width, but a 3-inch ruffle is what many custom workrooms use as their standard width. Try using a fabric remnant for the ruffle.

❂ Pillow fronts can be created from decorator fabrics, a needlepoint project, or an interesting piece of tapestry fabric. Sometimes you can splurge on fabric for the pillow front and select a less expensive coordinating fabric for the backing.

❂ Make pillows from your child's favorite T-shirts that are still in great shape but don't fit anymore.

❂ Pillows are perfect decorating accessories for kids' rooms. They make a bed an inviting place to curl up with a book. They can also be tossed on the floor for portable seating for visiting friends.

❂ Embellish a plain pillow top with ribbon trim, tassels, cording, hand or machine quilting, appliqué designs, patchwork, or antique or fabric-covered buttons.

❂ Pillows don't require much fabric, so you'll get more punch for your decorating dollar if you make several pillows from one yard of fabric.

❂ Search the bargain bins and remnant table for special buys on decorator fabric.

❂ Recycle your old pillows by discarding the existing pillow covers and making new covers to fit the forms.

❂ Make your own pillow forms with scraps of batting and fiberfill stuffing. From the batting, cut two outer layers 1 inch larger than pillow top. Cut four more pairs of layers, each 2 inches smaller than the previous pair. Separate and stack the layers by sizes into two piles with the largest layer on the bottom of each pile. Then place the two piles together with the smallest layers together in the center. Baste around the edges of the pillow to hold the layers in place. Wrap the bundle with another piece of batting and stitch closed. Fill out any empty pockets (such as the corners) with fiberfill.

Washing Quilts

What do you do when Grandma's quilt gets dirty? Cleaning these precious pieces of time is a challenge. Textile curators disapprove of the idea of washing or dry cleaning old quilts. This is great advice for museums and collectors of rare and valuable antique quilts. But many people purchase quilts from auctions, flea markets, and estate sales to use every day and washing them becomes a necessity. Here are some guidelines for washing your own quilts that are not of museum quality.

- Check the quilt to see if there are any large holes or tears. Repair these before beginning any cleaning process. Here is one way to repair a small tear or hole. (Others exist, and your local quilt store or library will have more information on repair methods.) Place a good-quality piece of tulle over the hole or tear on both the front and the back of the quilt. Carefully handstitch the pieces of tulle to the quilt surface; make your stitches as invisible as possible.

- Once repairs are complete, place the quilt in a top-loading washing machine. Set the dials for a large load and warm water. Add a small amount of detergent such as Orvis Paste or Ultra-Ivory

Decorating with Quilts

It's such a shame to hide a colorful quilt collection by keeping it tucked away and out of sight. So bring your quilts out to play as a decorative accent.

☼ Contemporary lines can be softened (both visually and texturally) with a few quilts tossed over chairs or covering a bed.

☼ Use a quilt as a table covering. Let the quilt drape off the sides and onto the floor.

☼ Fabric printed to look like a quilt (available in fabric and quilt stores) is great as a shower curtain—especially around a claw foot tub.

☼ A rolled-up quilt, placed in a beautiful basket and set in the hallway or guest room is handy for overnight guests.

dishwashing liquid to the water. These special detergents are available in quilt and grocery stores. Do not use commercial brands of laundry detergent.

- Fill the washing machine with water. Turn off the machine before it starts to agitate. With your hands, gently move the quilt around for several minutes.

- Use the spin cycle to remove the water. Allow the washer to fill again with clean rinse water. Again, do not allow the machine to agitate. With your hands, gently move the quilt around for several minutes.

- Spin again. If the quilt was extremely dirty, you may want to repeat the entire process.

- Spread a clean sheet (larger than the quilt) outdoors in a shaded area. Remove the quilt very carefully from the washer and lay it facedown on the sheet. Don't hang the quilt on a clothesline or over a fence because you risk damaging the quilt.

- When the quilt feels completely dry, bring it inside and drape it over a bed for a few days to be sure that it is thoroughly dry before you store it or put it to use.

※ Greet your guests as they travel to an upper level of your home by displaying a quilt over a banister. However, the stress of hanging can distort the shape of a quilt. Rotate quilts hung over a banister or on a wall to give the quilts a necessary rest.

※ Instead of a traditional holiday tree skirt, make a special quilt in red and green fabrics.

※ Rather than a framed picture, display a quilt over a sofa or behind a bed.

※ Toss a quilt over the back of a bench or fold and use it instead of a bench cushion.

※ Hang a quilt or two over a door that is always left open.

※ Fold several quilts and place them on the shelves of a bookcase or inside a pie chest.

☀ A decorative ladder placed in a corner is a perfect place to display colorful quilts.

☀ Place unmatched quilt squares casually around a room. These could be leftover from a project or bought secondhand.

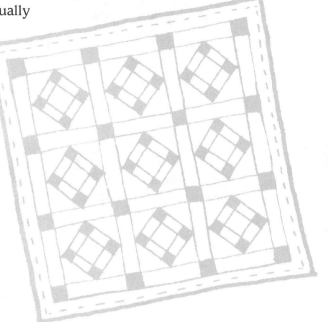

☀ Stack several quilts on top of each other at the foot of a bed. This is a great way to use worn quilts. Fold them so the best areas show on the outside. This way of displaying quilts is perfect for a guest room where the quilts won't be disturbed very often.

☀ Pieced quilt tops that have never been quilted drape nicely on a rod over windows and are great to use for shower curtains.

☀ A folded quilt placed over a large wooden headboard will soften the harsh lines of a bed.

☀ Use a quilt as a decorative daybed cover. Simply drape a quilt over the front edge across the seat and up over the bed frame. Add lots of pillows to make an inviting place to sit and relax.

☀ Incorporate the look of patchwork in ready-made table-cloths, shower curtains, or window treatments with fusible web and an assortment of fabric squares. Cut same-size squares that will fit the item you are decorat-ing. Apply paper-backed adhesive to the wrong side of the fabric squares; follow the manufacturer's instructions. Arrange the squares in a checkerboard fashion over the entire curtain or tablecloth and fuse in place.

Linens Old and New

Linens—napkins, towels, even handkerchiefs—offer many decorating options. Use them in nontraditional places for charming and creative accents.

Do's and Don'ts When Decorating with Quilts

Now that you're excited about decorating with your quilts, preserve them by following these common-sense suggestions.

- Never pin or nail a quilt to the wall; the nails could rust and leave permanent stains on the fabric. In addition, both pins and nails will leave holes in the quilt.

- Sew a muslin "sleeve" along the edges of a quilt for hanging. The sleeve needs to be wide enough for a rod to fit through. Don't sew tabs of fabric to the edges of the quilt as this will cause the quilt to pull at the hanging points and the quilt will become distorted.

- When draping quilts over wooden rods or pieces of furniture, make sure the wood has been treated with polyurethane to prevent it from staining the quilt.

- To store a quilt, roll it around a long cardboard tube (such as one that decorator fabric comes on) and cover it with a prewashed 100 percent cotton sheet. Don't store a quilt in a plastic bag because it locks in moisture that will destroy the contents.

- Before storing a quilt, make sure it is as free as possible from dust before you put it away.

⚙ Shop at flea markets and yard sales for old table linens, handkerchiefs, and dresser scarves for your projects.

⚙ Towels are a natural material for bathroom decorating. Wrap, staple, or glue towels to cover laundry baskets, wastebaskets, or even use as a sink skirt.

⚙ Embroidered napkins (either vintage or ones you made yourself) can be used as a handkerchief valance. Use as many napkins as necessary to fit the width of your window and hang them diagonally over an existing curtain rod. Overlap them for a fuller look.

Stamping Out Stains

Household linens and lace are subject to many stains. Following is a list of some of the most common stains and suggested remedies for them.

Candle Wax: Scrape off as much wax as possible with the dull edge of a knife. Place the item between two clean paper towels. Iron over the wax spot; the heat will draw the wax into the towel. Change the towels as the wax is absorbed.

Tea and Coffee: Gently rub glycerin into the stain. Hold the fabric tautly over the top of a bowl and pour boiling water onto the stain. When the stain is removed, wash the entire cloth by hand.

Scorches: Cut an onion in half and rub the cut side against the scorch. Soak the stain in cold water before laundering.

Ballpoint Pen Ink: Spray the ink stain with aerosol hair spray. Place a clean towel over the stained area and press gently. The hair spray will transfer the ink to the towel.

Red Wine: For a fresh stain, cover it with table salt, then rinse it with cold water. If the stain has dried, pour club soda onto the spot before laundering.

Lipstick: Gently rub a small amount of vegetable oil over the stain, then launder to remove the oil.

Rust: Mix one teaspoon of oxalic acid crystals (available in hardware stores) with one cup of distilled water. Pour this mixture over the rust spot and clean as usual.

Fruit Juice: Rinse the stain with cool water and clean as usual.

Cream or Milk: Rinse the spot with cool water and clean as usual. Never use hot water on protein stains.

Grease: Rub talcum powder into the grease spot to absorb the grease. Sponge off the powder before laundering. Lighter fluid will also dissolve greasy residue.

Mildew: Apply a solution of half hydrogen peroxide and half water to the spot, then launder.

Yellowing: Mix a paste of salt and lemon juice and apply a layer to the yellow area. Set it in the sun for 30 minutes.

Meat Juices: Soak the stain in cool water before cleaning. Never use hot water on protein stains.

☀ Curtain panels can easily be created with napkins or dishtowels with a few stitches. Overlap the linens, create a rod pocket, and add a few buttons. (See page 179 for complete instructions.)

☀ Stitch your collection of souvenir handkerchiefs or beautiful napkins into a unique coverlet. Don't despair if you don't have enough fancy handkerchiefs—add plain napkins to fill out the design. Or, for a custom coverlet, create your own "napkins" from fabrics of your choice.

☀ To make a simple lace tabletopper, arrange four Battenburg lace napkins into a square. Put the most decorative corners at the outside edge of the topper. Overlap the edges of the napkins slightly and stitch them together with a 1/4-inch seam allowance. Cover the seams with lengths of ribbon.

☀ Gather together a collection of old hand-embroidered towels and display them together in a bathroom or bedroom.

☀ Line a basket with antique hankies and fill it with pretty soaps to match the color scheme of your bathroom.

☀ Convert napkins into a colorful seat cover for bar stools. Place a napkin over the seat and gather each corner of the napkin together with a rubber band to secure the napkin over the seat. Cover the rubber bands with strips of fabric, cording, or ribbon.

☀ Use two 20-inch square cloth napkins to create a unique chair cover that will perfectly match the rest of the table decor. (Turn to page 204 for instructions for this project.)

☀ To create a whimsical and practical valance for the kitchen, select two complementary patterned dishtowels and stitch them together back to back; leave the top 3 inches open at the sides. Stitch across the width of the towel 1 inch and 3 inches down from the top edge to form the rod pocket. Insert a rod in the rod pocket.

Sheet Savvy

A new set of sheets will do wonders for a bedroom, creating a comfortable retreat from everyday hustle and bustle. In addition, sheets usually offer a large piece of

10 – Fabric Furnishings

fabric at a lower price than purchasing fabric by the yard. (Wait for white sales for even more savings.) You can use sheets to make curtains, table skirts, pillows, shower curtains, duvet covers, and more. Here are some tips to get you started.

❁ When working with sheets, be aware that many times the printed design is not placed in the same position on the sheets because the sheets are randomly cut to size. This may make it difficult to match the designs if fabric needs to be joined. The simplest solution is to select a sheet with a small allover design, a random print, or a stripe.

❁ To successfully decorate with sheets, buy all the sheets at the same time so the dye lots won't vary.

❁ Flat, rather than fitted, sheets usually provide more usable fabric.

❁ Mix and match prints and solids. Sheet manufacturers usually make their solid sheets to coordinate perfectly with their prints.

❁ Some sheets feature scalloped or trimmed edges and borders that can add extra design interest if the project is planned around them.

❁ The design on sheets continues from edge to edge including the selvages. This translates into a real timesaver because there is no need for side hems.

❁ In most cases, don't bother washing the sheets before making up the project—washing removes the sheen and sizing. However, do prewash your sheets if the finished item will be laundered regularly.

❁ When substituting flat sheets for 54-inch-wide fabric, estimate that a twin sheet equals $3^1/8$ yards, a full sheet equals $3^7/8$ yards, a queen equals $4^1/2$ yards, and a king equals $5^3/8$ yards.

HOW MUCH YARDAGE WILL I GET FROM A SHEET?

TWIN SHEET = $3^1/8$ YARDS

FULL SHEET = $3^7/8$ YARDS

QUEEN SHEET = $4^1/2$ YARDS

KING SHEET = $5^3/8$ YARDS

Sheet Success

Sheet designs are showing up on all types of ready-made merchandise from comforters to lamps to towels and rugs. For a great time-saving decorating approach, make the simplest items for your room and purchase the rest for a completely pulled-together look.

☀ You can use sheets anywhere in a home—not just the bedroom. They make very colorful seat covers, place mats, table runners, window treatments, decorative pillows, padded headboards, table skirts, and more.

☀ A decorative flat sheet is a quick furniture cover-up for an old worn sofa or chair. Tuck the sheet into the crevices for a more sculptured look. At the corners, tie the excess fabric together with ribbon or decorative cording.

☀ You can create a duvet cover by stitching two sheets together. Leave the top edge open for inserting your comforter. Attach hook-and-loop tape, buttons, snaps, self-fabric ties, or lengths of pretty ribbon across the top for closing. Note: If you plan to sleep with your duvet, use the end without the closing at the head of the bed because the buttons, snaps, or hook-and-loop tape may be uncomfortable to sleep with. (You'll find instructions on page 182 for a duvet cover.)

☀ Create a layered dust ruffle by covering box springs with a basic dust ruffle and then topping with a coordinating flat sheet one size smaller than the bed's size. Gather the corners of the sheet together and secure it in place with a piece of ribbon or a napkin ring.

☀ Use sheets to decorate a bathroom. The beautiful designs and colors found in sheets have enough visual interest to stand alone or coordinate with a nearby bedroom.

☀ Transform a plain flat sheet into a shower curtain by painting a whimsical design on the front in colors of your choice. If you're nervous about freehand sketching, use some of the wonderful stencils, rubber stamps, and block stamping products on the market. Add some evenly spaced buttonholes or grommets along the top edge of the sheet. Note: A purchased shower curtain is approximately 72 by 72 inches. However, don't worry about trimming the sheet to a specific dimension. The fuller the shower curtain is, the more luxurious it looks when installed.

☀ Drape a full-sized flat sheet over a round accent table. Tuck under the ends for the "hem." The resulting look is rich and poufed. If you don't want the poufed look and would prefer a more tailored table skirt, cut away the excess fabric with pinking shears to avoid hemming.

☀ Decorating accessories such as table runners, place mats, and napkins can be made economically from sheets.

☀ Slip a king-sized pillowcase over the back of a dining room chair for an instant slipcover. For an added embellishment, make a bow from fabric or ribbon and attach it to the back of the chair cover.

☀ Make a fabric-covered headboard to match your bed ensemble using a sheet from the collection.

☀ Use three full-sized flat sheets to create a soft canopy behind your bed. You'll also need three towel rings. Attach the towel rings to the wall as follows: one centered above the bed and the others slightly above each side of the bed. Gather the top edges of all three sheets together and pull them through the top ring; arrange the ends in a rosette. Allow the center sheet to hang straight down and drape the side sheets through the side rings.

A Case for Pillows

Pillowcases are a perfect choice when decorating your bedroom. Many sheet designs offer coordinating options that will make perfect accent pillows. Two of these projects require very little stitching—and one is completely no-sew!

- Create reversible pillowcases for inexpensive and quick-changeable decorating. Turn one purchased pillowcase wrong side out and stuff it inside another pillowcase; line up the seams and top edges. Sew buttonholes through both pillowcases along one side of the finished hem (fig. 1). Handstitch buttons to the other side of finished hem; make sure buttons and buttonholes are lined up. Then stitch another set of buttons directly behind the first set (fig. 2). Hand tack the two pillow-

Figure 1   Figure 2

cases together at each bottom corner. Turn them inside out. Insert the pillow; button the top edges of the pillowcase together. When you want a change, turn the pillowcase wrong side out to display the other side. Note: Use this pillowcase strictly as a decorative treatment to avoid excessive laundering.

- Make a throw pillow from a standard-sized pillowcase (20 by 30 inch) by making six machine-made buttonholes in the hem area. Center 3 each on the front and back, making sure they line up on top of each other when the pillowcase lies flat (fig. 1). Fold over the open end of the pillowcase about 10 inches and mark button positions in the top layer of the pillow through the buttonholes (fig. 2). Sew a decorative button at each mark (fig. 3). Place a 20-inch pillow form in the pillowcase and button the edge through the corre- sponding button- holes (fig. 4).

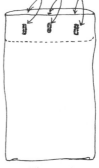

Figure 1

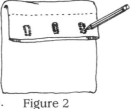

Figure 2

Figure 3

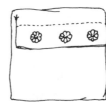

Figure 4

- The easiest pillow to make starts with a standard-sized pillowcase. Insert an 18- or 20-inch pillow (fig. 1) into the opening (make sure the pillow "fills" the interior space). Then gather the open ends together and secure with a rubber band. Cover the band with a contrasting fabric strip, cording, or ribbon (fig. 2). Arrange the gath- ered fabric into a rosette (fig. 3).

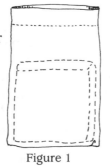

Figure 1

Figure 2

Figure 3

10 – Fabric Furnishings

✤ To make an easy window treatment, use two twin-sized sheets cut to the desired length (plus a little extra for the hem). Hem the bottom cut edge with iron-on hem tape. Gather the corners at the top edges together and tie them to a decorative rod with lengths of ribbon.

✤ Install a decorative rod over the window and from it hang colorful pillowcases with decorative clips for a no-fail window treatment.

✤ To make a unique window treatment, use two twin-sized sheets that have been cut and hemmed to the desired length. Stamp a design randomly over the surface. Insert four grommets along the top edge of each sheet; make sure they are evenly spaced. Install decorative brass hooks above the window frame and hang the curtains by the grommets.

✤ Make an easy two-tone swag window treatment with two twin- or full-sized flat sheets (for a double window). For added interest, select two coordinating sheets. Mount a rod above the window frame and slip a curtain rod through the two wide top hems of each sheet. Hang the rod, then slide the sheets toward the center of it. Cross them and drape them over the rods at the opposite corners.

✤ For another window treatment, cut and hem two twin-sized sheets to the desired length. Insert eight grommets evenly across the top edge of each sheet. Cut a length of cording for each panel that is $1^{1}/_{2}$ times longer than the finished width. Lace the cording through the grommets as follows: make a large single knot at one end of the cord. Beginning at the outside corner of each sheet, insert the cording from front to back; pull it until the knot is against the grommet. Bring the cording over the top edge to the front of the sheet and insert it through the next grommet. Continue in this manner until all the grommets are used. When all the grommets are laced, make a large single knot on the end of the cord to secure it.

11 Collections

For some people, collecting is a hobby. For others, it's a passion that is so strong, it's almost obsessive. If you are a collector, you'll find that decorating with all of your treasures adds a personal touch and a special coziness to your home that no interior decorator could accomplish.

Public Display of Collections

Part of the fun of collecting is displaying your finds. Here are some ideas for you if you can't decide where to display your collections.

- Large areas of wall space are a logical starting point, but don't forget less obvious places: over the bed, along a narrow hallway or stairway, or even on window sills.

- If the items are going to be viewed by people who are likely to be standing, hang the pictures at a standing person's eye level. Otherwise, hang the items at the eye level of someone who is seated.

- Display your favorite collections in a room where the most people are going to see them (probably the living room).

- Use a round table to display your collections. Place the table in a corner, add a floor-length table covering, and adorn the surface with your treasures.

Collective Thoughts

What you collect says something about you. If you aren't a collector yet, but you'd like to become one, here's a list of ideas for collections that may help you decide what's right for you.

advertising art
antique telephones
autographs
bells
birdhouses
birth announcements
bottles
brooms
butterflies
cars

ceramic tiles
certificates
children's portraits
clocks
coins
cowboy boots
decoys
diplomas
doorknobs
fire fighting items
game boards
hats
immigration papers
kitchen utensils
license plates
marionettes
masks
matchbooks

measuring devices
   (rulers, yardsticks, etc.)
miniature chairs
miniature quilts
movie posters
musical instruments
old eyeglasses
Old West gear
period items
   (1950s, 1960s, etc.)
picture frames
plates
pocket watches
political bumper stickers
postcards
primitive lighting
primitive signs

radios
records
rustic benches
seashells
sewing tools
ship's wheels
signs
small drawers
spoons

sports memorabilia
stamps
teacups/teapots
telephones
theater programs/ticket
   stubs
thimbles
ticket stubs from
   sporting events or
   concerts
tiny buildings
toy trains
Valentine's Day cards
vintage advertisements
vintage children's
   storybooks
vintage fruit labels
weapons
wedding invitations
wine labels and corks
wooden sleds
wristwatches
yard tools

❋ Create a seasonal display of your collectibles and change it with the season. Display these items on a fireplace mantel, a shelf, or a tabletop.

❋ To have continuity in your collections, choose items within a specific color scheme. Collect items to go with the room where they will be displayed.

❋ Add and take away pieces until you are pleased with the arrangement. Your display will look better if you don't try to cram everything into one place.

❋ Arrange small stacking tables in an unused corner to display your collection of pottery.

❋ Place a flat basket on your coffee table and fill it with some of your favorite items.

❋ Gather together all of your crystal and glass candlesticks and place them on a table that needs some sparkle. For even more impact, set the candlesticks on a large mirror.

❋ Personalize your collection by interspersing items that are characteristic of you, your family, and your friends with your displays. Perhaps you could display old family photos or items made especially for you by a special friend.

11 - Collections

☀ When arranging items on a wall, start with the three largest objects; then fill in the space between them with smaller items. It may be helpful to sketch the arrangement on paper or lay the items out on the floor to get a better idea of the overall look before hammering away. Or better yet, tape together several large pieces of paper and arrange the items on the paper. When you are pleased with the arrangement, trace around the shapes and mark a spot on the paper where each nail or hanger should be placed. Then tape the paper to the wall, hammer each nail through the appropriate mark and pull the paper off the nails. Hang the art or collectibles in the appropriate places.

☀ Hang large items over a sofa—not because smaller pieces will look lost in such a large space but because they cannot be examined without kneeling on the sofa. Large pieces can be viewed from a distance.

☀ Don't mount items too high above furnishings, as pictures and furniture pieces should appear related. A good test for height is to have a tall friend sit on the sofa. Mark the wall about 3 inches above his or her head. Use this mark as the lowermost edge of any framed picture.

☀ Use peg molding strips installed at mantel height around the room to display your favorite hats. Intersperse dried flowers among the hats to add even more texture.

☀ For an eye-pleasing wall display, create a geometric shape with the outer items of the grouping. Achieve cohesiveness by hanging items close together so they appear to be a unit; make sure one item in the grouping doesn't overpower the others.

☀ If you change your displays often, reuse existing nail holes by selecting a new object that is similar in size to the previous one.

☀ "Frame" your collection with a wall border that complements your collection. For example, select a sewing-themed border print to surround sewing-related collectibles.

☀ Make your hat collection into a valance. Change your hats with new ones as you want—or display hats for different seasons. (See page 200 for complete instructions for this project.)

☀ Display old photographs and postcards under a glass-covered tabletop. For added impact, make a floor-length table cover, add a topper with lavish fringe, and then scatter photos across the table surface. Secure everything in place with a protective glass top.

☀ For a more permanent underglass display, consider using decoupage to apply photos to the underside of a glass surface. (See page 206 for complete instructions for this project.)

☀ A wreath makes a perfect showcase for small collectibles such as jewelry. Attach seldom-worn costume jewelry to the wreath with bits of ribbon.

☀ Decorate a wreath with mementos collected from a recent family outing. Have each family member contribute something meaningful to the wreath. The result will be a timeless treasure.

☀ Use mismatched picture frames to display flat collectibles: photos, certificates, diplomas, artwork, vintage fruit labels, postcards, wine labels, and so on.

☀ Frame three-dimensional objects in shadowboxes.

☀ Use assorted shelves to display items too large to fit in shadowboxes.

☀ Ledges are ideal for displaying plates, dishes, cups, and other narrow collectibles.

☀ Hang framed objects from a coat rack with ribbon.

☀ Use a folding screen to show off your treasures. Attach shelves at different levels on each section. (You can learn how to create a screen with shelves on page 200.)

☀ Use interesting doorknobs collected from antique stores or flea markets to display items such as framed pictures. Secure a doorknob to the wall; wrap a pretty ribbon around the wire hanger of the picture and tie a bow over the doorknob.

☀ Arrange your collectibles in odd-numbered groups (3, 5, 7 and so on).

Display Do's and Don'ts

To preserve your treasures for years to come, take some extra time to ensure their longevity.

• Do use high-quality mats and backing boards when framing valuable photos and other documents. Use only acid-free materials and keep the items out of direct sunlight. To preserve very valuable documents, place them in an acid-free folder and store them in a dark place with low humidity.

• Don't display items next to an air conditioner, lamp, or heating unit.

• Don't store items in areas of your house that are prone to dampness (bathrooms, cellars, laundry rooms).

• Do use proper picture hooks and/or wire to hang framed items securely.

❀ Vary the heights of the items when displaying your collectibles. Use wooden boxes, dishes, books, or cigar boxes to lift some items above the others.

❀ Diversify texture by using shiny surfaces to display rough and flat objects.

CAN ITEMS FROM
DIFFERENT
COLLECTIONS
BE GROUPED
TOGETHER?

❀ Trail a ribbon through a stack of books to make the arrangement a little more friendly.

❀ Don't overaccessorize. Cluster a few favorite items on a table or bureau for maximum impact.

❀ For a relaxed, lived-in look, leave piles of books out on coffee tables, mantels, and of course, in bookshelves.

Tablescapes

Tabletops are perfect areas to display cherished collections. When you are creating a tablescape, think of creating a still life. Here are some simple guidelines to create your own arrangement.

❀ Choose items that you truly love to display on a tabletop. Often the simplest items create the most interesting displays.

❀ Balance the size and scale of the objects with the surface area on which the items will be displayed.

❀ Three or more objects of the same type become a grouping and will make an attractive tablescape.

❀ Very different items can be unified by color, shape, and the periods in which they were made.

❀ For table collections, arrange the items so the larger collectibles are toward the back of the table and the smaller ones are in front.

❀ Add and subtract items until you find a grouping that is pleasing to your eye.

❀ Aim for balance with the items you are displaying. However, balance doesn't mean symmetry.

11 – Collections

❁ Don't overcrowd a tabletop. Showcase a few items at a time.

❁ Repetition of a single item is interesting to look at. For example, mingle several items that are the same shape (round, square, triangular) with other pieces.

❁ Look beyond the tabletop for display areas. Fill the large area under the table with large items such as hatboxes or baskets filled with dried flowers.

❁ Introduce fabrics in the tablescape. Arrange the fabric into attractive folds for added dimension.

12 Storage Solutions

A home can never have enough shelves and closets. However, these traditional storage options are not the only places to use for storage. Consider these suggestions.

Stow It with Style

Hide those items no more. Here are some ways to store them in plain sight.

- Use window sills to hold flower vases and small glass trinkets.

- Install open shelves above a door, sink, or window. Display colorful glassware, interesting dishes, or even a few pieces of your favorite pottery.

- When selecting small appliances for your kitchen, consider choosing the type that can be mounted underneath cabinets to free up precious counter space.

- Use every available surface for storage, including ceilings. Install overhead pot racks, wall grids, and plate rails.

- Consider landings, alcoves, foyers, and the space below stairways for storage possibilities.

- Provide see-through wire drawers for your children to store toys in. These will make it easier for your children to find their favorite playthings.

❊ With just a few 1- by 2-inch boards, some nails, and some paint, you can build a stylish towel ladder (not for climbing). Lean the finished project against the wall in the bathroom for a unique and functional storage solution. Hint: Secure the top and bottom of the ladder to the wall and floor with sticky-backed hook-and-loop fastener tape.

Clutter Busters

You won't dread saying (or hearing) "Clean up your room!" when you utilize some of these suggestions to dispose of your clutter.

❊ Make use of every inch of a room— install peg molding strips on a wall or behind a door to stretch the space in a room.

❊ Use a coated wire grid to hang mugs and utensils in a kitchen area—use S-hooks to grip the handles.

❊ Increase access to storage space in kitchen cabinets by using tiered lazy Susans or step-shelves.

❊ To increase storage space in an already cramped bathroom, stow items under the sink and hide the clutter with a colorful sink skirt.

❊ Hang a peg rack in your bathroom or beside your dressing table to use to hang jewelry.

❊ In the bathroom, use peg racks or individual hooks to hang everyday towels.

❊ Stack graduated sizes of suitcases and use them as a bedside stand. Fill the suitcases with seldom-used treasures.

❊ Use the inside of cabinet doors for storing spices, paper goods, and other small kitchen items. Scour specialty stores for unique racks and shelves for out-of-the-way storage options.

❊ In your child's room, suspend a small toy hammock from the ceiling and fill it with a stuffed toy collection.

☀ Install shelving about 8 to 12 inches below the ceiling in a hallway and store your books and collectibles on it. This practical approach to storage draws your eye up into an otherwise dead space and makes the hallway seem larger.

☀ Store cooking utensils on a wall to free up precious countertop and drawer space.

HOW CAN I ELIMINATE CLUTTER?

☀ The back of a door is a perfect place to store. Add hooks, grids, spice racks, and shoe bags to hold accessories, art materials, small toys, and yes, even shoes!

☀ Utilize empty spaces for additional storage. For example, use the area under a bed to store seldom-used items— arts-and-crafts supplies, wrapping paper, and seasonal decorations. Don't forget to use a dust ruffle to hide the boxes.

☀ Build a platform bed with drawers built in along the sides and shelves incorporated into the headboard.

☀ Children's rooms are challenging to find adequate storage places. A toy chest, an open closet with plenty of shelves, or even a corner cupboard provide plenty of options for toys, books, and clothing. Install shelves slightly out of reach for collectibles that won't be used often.

☀ Smaller items can be stored in cardboard closet organizers and placed on closet shelves. Remember to label each container so you know what is in it.

☀ Build window seats with lift-up tops for extra seating and maximum storage.

☀ Install drawers in the toe-kick space under your kitchen cabinets for trays, cookie tins, even place mats.

☀ Use kitchen cabinets for storage all through the house—in the hallway, the bathroom, the sewing room, and so on. To save money, use stock cabinets available at do-it-yourself centers.

☀ Empty corners are spaces just crying to be used for storage. Build or buy triangular hutches or baker's racks and fill them with interesting items.

12 – Storage Solutions

Out of Sight

Use your imagination to adapt unusual items (found or purchased) as creative storage receptacles.

☼ Hang personalized mailboxes near the doorway so that your family members will have a place to keep their hats, gloves, and keys. This is especially good for school-age kids to keep all of their school materials together.

☼ Transform empty coffee cans, potato chip cylinders, and other containers into great-looking storage boxes by covering them with fabric, corrugated paper, twine, or wallpaper.

☼ Create your own instant storage space with a plastic garbage can and a round piece of wood. Use the garbage can as the base and the round piece of wood as the top. Fill the garbage can with seasonal items (for example, sweaters or holiday ornaments). Disguise the "table" by covering it with a round tablecloth.

☼ Create one-of-a-kind decorative storage boxes by decorating the surface with stickers or illustrations from wrapping paper, greeting cards, magazines, or postcards. Almost any smooth surface can be covered with this technique. First, cut out individual motifs with cuticle or embroidery scissors and arrange them on the surface. Adhere the cutouts to the surface with decoupage liquid (available at craft stores). Make sure there are no wrinkles under the cutouts. Wipe off excess glue and allow the surface to dry before covering it with several coats of decoupage liquid. Allow the box to dry between coats.

In the Closet

Every inch counts when making the closet space in your house work for you and all of your belongings. If you use the space you have to its best potential, more space seems to miraculously appear. Here are some ideas to consider.

☼ Sliding and bifold doors are the least efficient type of doors to choose when planning your closets. A swing-style door will allow you to attach a mirror to the interior surface or hang accessories.

❀ Invest in colorful plastic hangers for a pleasing and uniform appearance in your closet.

HOW CAN I BEST USE CLOSET SPACE?

❀ Thin out the clothes in your closet to create space. Get rid of items that you haven't worn in a year or two.

❀ Sort clothing into like groups: skirts, blouses, slacks, dresses, and so on. Then create subgroups within the like groups: i.e., dressy blouses and casual blouses. When you hang the items in a closet, they should all be hung facing the same direction.

❀ For your accessories, purchase plastic containers for individual items. These containers come in different sizes to accommodate many different-sized accessories.

❀ Multilevel storage is the main key to closet organization. Stacking drawers are perfect for this; you can purchase them as you need them.

Shelve It!

Shelves are a wonderful way to increase floor space by providing an area to store collectibles as well as necessities.

❀ Enliven existing shelves by painting them bright and interesting colors. Then trim the edges with lace, rope, decorative cording, or colorful thumbtacks.

Closet Sense

When planning your closet space, keep these guidelines in mind.

- Hang clothes rods at least 12 inches away from the back wall of the closet.

- For double-hanging rods, install the top rod approximately 82 inches above the floor and the lower rod approximately 41 inches off the floor.

- When hanging only a single rod, install it 63 to 72 inches above the floor. If you want to use shoe racks below it, position the rod to keep garments from touching the racks.

- Space shelves according to what will be stored on them; include 2 to 3 inches of room above the top item.

❋ Install open shelves above a door, sink, or window. This is a great way to display interesting and unmatched objects that you can't live without.

❋ Shelves on the wall are ideal places for storing plates, dishes, cups, and other narrow pieces.

❋ Use a child-sized bench as an inexpensive bedside bookshelf.

❋ The traditional way to display books is standing on their ends on shelves. Consider laying the books flat (spines out) so you can add more accessories or a photo or two on top of the books.

❋ Install floor-to-ceiling shelves or racks over the toilet tank, and place colorful towels, soaps, votive candles, pretty containers filled with potpourri, and baskets.

❋ A surprising place to hang several shelves is inside a window frame. Fill the shelves with colorful and multi-sized glasses, plants, or fresh flowers.

❋ In your child's room, install different-colored shelves at different heights. Adult-level shelves could store and display fragile toys while child-level shelves could be used for everyday toys.

The Care and Cleaning of Baskets

To extend the life of your baskets, you should care for them properly.

• Clean your baskets with a gentle sponging or by lightly brushing them with an artist's hog hair brush.

• Every few years, spray baskets lightly with a light furniture oil.

• On a regular basis, mist the baskets with water so they won't become brittle. Don't spray them too heavily or too often, or mold will become a problem.

☼ Add some Shaker-style peg shelving around the perimeter of the room. Not only does the shelf serve as a display area, but it acts as a visual link that leads the eye around the room. When placing the shelf, don't cut the room in half by hanging it exactly in the middle of the wall. (Learn how to make this project on page 199.)

☼ Use shelves to display your collection of glass- and crystal-stemmed glasses. Select several stemware racks and place them around the room. The top of the shelf is a perfect place to put glass candle holders.

Basket Case

Baskets have long been a decorating favorite. They come in many shapes and sizes and are perfect for holding all sorts of items. Let's go through the house, room by room, and discover some exciting ways to use baskets in decorating.

In the Bathroom

- Store towels and pretty soaps for your guests. Intersperse shampoo, lotion, and maybe even a candle. All of this says "Welcome" in a big way.
- Use small baskets as perfect potpourri containers.

In the Kitchen

- Place a medium-sized basket with unripened fruit in front of a window.
- Serve rolls, bread, or biscuits in a lined basket. Use a brightly colored napkin that depicts the theme of the season to line the basket.

In the Dining Room

- Wrap silverware in napkins and then arrange them in a large basket. This idea is great for a buffet dinner.
- Use a basket as a container for a seasonal centerpiece. Fill it with colorful fruit in summer, gourds in fall, fresh flowers in spring, and different-sized candles in winter.

In the Living Room

- Place small baskets around a room when entertaining and fill them with nuts and candies.

Continued

- Fill a large basket with wood or kindling and place it on your fireplace hearth (although not too close to the burning fire).
- Hang a grouping of baskets on the wall or from an exposed beam for added texture.
- Keep a basket full of magazines beside your favorite reading chair.
- Arrange some baskets on their bottoms, some on their sides, and intersperse other collectibles for added interest.
- Add color to your room by arranging balls of colorful yarn in a basket.

In a Nursery or Child's Room

- Fill baskets with lotions, powder, and pins.
- Place some small baskets in a drawer to keep rolled-up socks, T-shirts, and other garments organized and handy.
- Use a large basket to hold a collection of stuffed animals.

In the Hall

- Keep a basket near the door and place your keys in it upon your return. No longer will you have frantic searches for your keys when it's time to leave.
- Use a large rectangular basket for important outgoing mail.
- Place a small basket near the phone and keep it supplied with pens, pencils, and writing paper for those all-important messages.

Around the House

- Use a basket to hold your garden tools and gloves. They will always be handy for your gardening tasks.
- Use baskets to hold your cassettes and video-tapes.
- Leave expensive, handmade baskets their original color. However, feel free to decorate your inexpensive baskets with paint, decals, stencils, and sponge or spatter painting. After decorating, seal the basket with a clear coat of varnish.

- Use one basket in your home office as your "in-basket" and another for your "out-basket." Consider using small baskets to hold your paper clips, pencils, rubber bands, and stamps.
- Hide ugly plastic planters inside pretty baskets.

13 *Children's Rooms*

*I*f you are decorating for the first addition to your family or if you're an old pro, consider these inexpensive options before you embark on this decorating endeavor.

Nursery Time

You have plenty of time to plan this room. Have fun and be creative when making your decorating decisions.

☼ To decorate children's rooms that will grow with them, resist the temptation to use infantile motifs such as little ducks and cuddly bunnies. Instead, select geometric shapes or stripes that will be suitable for the children as they get older. The duckies and bunnies can be included in the decor via removable wall stickers and stuffed animals.

☼ To create a room in which to grow, select neutral colors for the walls and floor covering. The color scheme will develop as fabric accessories are added to the room.

☼ A wallpaper border adds instant coziness to a nursery.

☼ Removable wall appliqués are the perfect choice when decorating a nursery because they allow you to redecorate easily as the child gets older.

☼ Make a bassinet skirt from two pairs of café curtains. Stitch them together at the sides and then insert a length of elastic through the top casing. To determine the length of elastic needed, stretch the elastic snugly around the bassinet's perimeter; allow a little extra for overlap.

❁ Glue colorful wooden balls (at least 1 inch in diameter) to the base of an inexpensive lamp. Select colors that coordinate with the rest of the fabric furnishings.

❁ For a unique wall decoration in a nursery, frame beautiful illustrations from the pages of a storybook.

❁ When decorating a nursery or a child's room, select washable fabrics instead of fabrics that require dry cleaning.

Kid's Stuff

Boys and girls have very specific ideas of what they like. Depending on the ages of your children, solicit their help—there are plenty of ways for them to become involved!

❁ Develop a decorating theme according to your child's interest. Cars, trains, dolls, and animals are all themes that are easy to find as accessory motifs.

❁ Decorating your child's room is easy with the wide variety of children's fabrics available from several fabric manufacturers.

❁ Girls' rooms don't have to be pink and boys' rooms don't have to be blue. Break this stereotype by choosing any color of the rainbow that your child likes.

❁ When purchasing furniture for a child's room, think ahead. Perhaps your youngster doesn't need a desk yet, but a few years from now a matching desk will come in handy for homework assignments.

❁ Loft beds increase floor space in children's rooms.

❁ Keep window treatments simple. A shirred valance over mini-blinds may be all you need.

❁ Consider purchasing a bed with drawers under it. The drawers make what would otherwise have been wasted space into optimal storage.

☀ Cover several homasote boards (available at home improvement stores) with colorful felt. Felt comes in small rectangles but is also available in a wide variety of colors by the yard. Fasten the board to the wall with wall anchors. From leftover felt, cut numbers, letters, and shapes for a personalized felt board your child will have fun with. (See page 191 for complete instructions.)

☀ Paint clouds or stars on the ceiling and rainbows on the walls. Or buy sponges in the shapes of animals or letters and cover the walls with these images with only a little bit of acrylic paint.

☀ Hang different-colored shelves at different heights around the room. The lowest shelf can do double duty as a study desk.

☀ Pillows are the perfect decorating accessory for children's rooms—both on a bed or for seating on the floor.

13 – Children's Rooms

❋ Paint the floor to go with the color scheme of the room. Geometric shapes are easy to paint and add a fun decorative touch.

❋ Include chalkboards and bulletin boards when planning wall treatments. With special chalkboard paint, you can create a large chalkboard directly on the wall. (Learn how on page 199.)

❋ Make a chalkboard door by applying several coats of chalkboard paint directly to the door front. Trim the outer edges in a semi-gloss or high-gloss latex paint for easy cleaning.

❋ Select shelving that is versatile enough so the height can be changed to accommodate the child's growth. Tinier folks need their possessions at a lower level than their older siblings do.

❋ Install a shelf around the entire perimeter of the room to support the track for a working toy train. Imagine the fun your child will have watching the locomotive navigate the natural "terrain" of the room. For added interest, paint a countryside scene or add a colorful wall border behind the train.

☀ An old, pull-down, vinyl window shade makes a great temporary chalkboard for a child's room. Trim off any frayed edges and paint the shade with special chalkboard paint. When dry, hang the shade in a convenient place in your child's room. When not in use, the shade can be rolled up out of the way.

☀ Divide closet space in half by hanging two rods: one at a child's level and another one higher up to hang seasonal or seldom-worn clothing.

☀ Frame a page or the cover of a favorite comic book for an inexpensive, yet colorful, wall decoration.

☀ Use your child's hat collection as a valance and change the hats with the season as his or her interests change. (See page 200 for instructions.)

☀ Paint a racetrack (shaped like a large figure eight) directly on the floor of your child's room. Add interesting scenery and potential "pit stops" along the way to encourage an imaginative race.

☀ Provide see-through wire drawers to store toys. These will make it easier for your children to find—and put away— their favorite toys.

☀ Suspend a small hammock from the ceiling and fill it with a stuffed toy collection.

☀ Hang a jersey of a favorite player or team on the wall or window with a decorative rod, brackets, and finials.

13 - Children's Rooms

☼ Cut a length of picket fence to fit the top portion of a sashed window and mount it (points down) from the top of the window frame. Embellish the fence with cheerful silk flowers or paint, stamp, or stencil your child's favorite designs directly to the surface.

☼ Make pillows from your child's favorite T-shirts that are in great shape but don't fit anymore.

☼ For a child's room, write the words of your favorite nursery rhyme or bedtime story on the wall.

14 Master the Bath

Your decorating efforts will certainly be admired in the bathroom. Here are some ideas your family and guests will appreciate.

Bathing Beauty

☀ Keep these ideas in mind when you choose colors for your bathroom. Pink and peach are colors that give everyone a natural, healthy glow; yellow produces just the opposite effect. Pink and peach can also cheer you up and help you release tension. White gives a clean and sterile impression. In addition, the oldest of bathrooms look years younger when everything is painted white. If you need to have some help waking up in the mornings, you may want to select a bright red and green color scheme.

☀ If you plan to sell your house sometime in the future, you may want to select tiles for the bath in neutral colors such as white, gray, beige, taupe, peach, or ivory. To add your personal touch, decorate the bath in colors that you love. Select a wonderful shower curtain and accent the room with towels and accessories.

☀ Line a basket with antique hankies and fill the basket with pretty soaps to match the color scheme of the bath.

☀ A basket is also a practical place to store rolled-up hand towels and add more color to your bathroom. Not only is it practical, but it is a color solution as well.

☀ Stencil or stamp a design on a clothes hamper to match the wall decoration.

☀ You can change your bathroom color scheme frequently if you start with a shower curtain that has many colors. A new color scheme can be developed by changing towels, rugs, and various accessories.

☀ Use peg racks or individual hooks to hang everyday towels.

☀ Make use of colorful mugs, vases, and dishes to hold your toothbrush, toothpaste, and makeup brushes.

☀ Instead of replacing your old tub, have it professionally refinished in an exciting new color.

☀ When selecting wallpaper or borders for your bathroom, don't limit yourself to the sample books that focus on bathrooms. Look for an unusual theme that shows your creativity (and your sense of humor).

☀ For an inexpensive wall covering, provide your guests with different-colored permanent markers and have them write messages, sayings, or whatever crosses their minds on your bathroom wall. This colorful and inexpensive alternative to wallpaper is a real attention getter!

☀ If you can't replace your old toilet, camouflage it with a new toilet seat.

☀ You'll be pleasantly surprised at how a new faucet and fittings will make an old sink look new.

☀ If you don't have a cabinet to hide unsightly plumbing pipes, make a colorful skirt for the sink and attach it with hook-and-loop tape. Use this same skirt idea on an old-fashioned tub to soften the look of the room.

☀ Plush towels add a layer of luxury to an ordinary bath. Wait for annual white sales to stock up. Why not select colors that will mix and match to create different looks?

☀ Use the wall space in your bathroom to display your favorite collectibles like teacups, vases, or old plates.

☀ Glue lace trim to the edges of the shelves inside your medicine cabinet.

☀ Towel racks don't have to be traditional. Use decorative curtain rods and finials, unique hooks, or even out-stretched hands. If you look at found objects in a new way, you'll discover many good ideas for towel racks.

☀ Instead of a traditional window treatment, hang a piece of stained glass at a window. When the sun shines through it, colors will dance across the room.

☀ Try using outdoor furniture in the bathroom. It is made to withstand moisture and will be right at home in a bathroom.

14 – Master the Bath

☀ Make a plain muslin shower curtain and then paint a whimsical design on the front in colors of your choice. Or if you're nervous about freehand sketching, use some of the stencils, rubber stamps, and block-stamping products on the market.

☀ If you have ceramic-tiled walls in the bath and shower area and want a new look, consider replacing a row or two of existing tiles with a different color.

☀ Resurface a deteriorating vanity with small tiles arranged in an interesting mosaic design for a brand-new finish.

☀ An eye-catching floor mat for any bathroom can be quickly made by knotting colorful strips of ribbon around the outer edges of a sisal rug. Simply cut an assortment of ribbons into 10-inch lengths. Use an awl or crochet hook to push each ribbon between the fibers along the mat edge. Tie the ribbons into square knots.

☀ A unique container for holding toiletries or magazines is a wooden or terra-cotta window box—the kind usually used for plants. Paint or decorate the window box with ceramic tiles to match your decor. Set the finished box on the back of the toilet for room-saving storage. (To find out how to make a tile-covered box, turn to page 207.)

☀ Add a fabric canopy over an old-fashioned freestanding tub. Install a plant hanger on the ceiling above the center of the tub. Arrange fabric so that it reaches from the floor on one side edge of the tub, through the ceiling hook, and down to the floor at the opposite side.

☀ Monogram your bathroom towels.

☀ An interesting way to present towels to your overnight guests is to use two different-colored, but coordinating, bath-sized towels and a tasseled tieback (available in fabric stores). Gather one end of a towel and place it behind a wall-mounted towel bar. Then gather the other end of the towel and bring it up in front of the towel bar to meet the first end. The gathered areas should match exactly. Tie the ends together above the towel bar using the tasseled tieback. Arrange the flounce attractively.

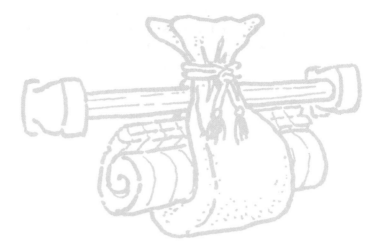

Finally, roll up the second towel and place it inside the lower loop of the hanging towel (the way a stork is pictured holding a baby in a blanket).

Too Close for Comfort?

Don't despair over a tiny bathroom. Learn to use every available inch within those four walls. Act as if you never realized that bathroom was small to begin with and do what you want!

☀ Build some shelves over the shower.

☀ Install floor-to-ceiling shelves or racks over the toilet tank and place colorful towels, soaps, and baskets (holding all your necessary toiletries) on the open shelves.

☀ Don't worry about painting your bathroom a dark color or using a large print in the wallpaper. (The room is small enough as it is and the visual room-expansion tricks you can do with paint and wallpaper are useless here.) Dark colors and wonderfully elaborate wallpaper will create a sense of drama.

☀ Use the largest mirror you can find in the tiniest of bathrooms. Properly spaced mirrors can make a small bathroom look twice as large. Hang two different-sized mirrors opposite each other for maximum magnification.

14 - Master the Bath

☀ A peg-rail shelf will help keep a small bathroom free of clutter by supplying a space for storing toiletries as well as a place to hang towels or other necessities.

☀ If you are replacing a bathroom floor, lay the floor tiles diagonally to give the illusion of more space.

15 Suite Dreams

Your bedroom should be the coziest and most comfortable room in your house, a haven from the harsh realities of day-to-day living. To make it special, try some of these tips. Be sure to also refer to chapters 3–5 for ideas about paint, wallpaper, curtains, and furniture. In fact, you'll find ideas to inspire your bedroom decorating project throughout the book.

☀ To evoke a peaceful feeling in a bedroom, select a shade of green because it is associated with comfort, quietness, and relaxation. Blues and purples are also calming. Pinks and peaches are warm and inviting.

☀ Indulge yourself and all your senses with luxury. Sight, sound, touch, and smell should all be considered when creating a personal retreat. Keep your favorite cassettes or compact disks handy, light a scented candle, and keep a collection of pillows on the bed.

☀ A new set of sheets will do wonders, setting the stage for a comfortable retreat. This minimum investment will produce maximum results.

☀ A profusion of pillows and cushions adds instant warmth, comfort, and coziness. Rearrange them when you want a different look. Mix and match fabrics, shapes, and sizes when piling on this layer of luxury.

15 – Suite Dreams

☀ Add a fabric-covered or decoratively painted folding screen to any corner of the room. This colorful addition can serve double or even triple duty—to camouflage unattractive areas of the room, act as extra insulation in drafty corners, or provide some privacy for a dressing area. (See pages 188 and 189 for folding screen instructions.)

☀ Include a comfortable chair in your bedroom for cuddling up with a good book and forgetting about the rest of the world (at least for a few chapters).

☀ Make a cozy throw or quilt for snuggling. Keep it handy on the end of the bed or on your reading chair.

☀ Install as plush a carpet as your budget allows for the feeling of luxury.

HOW CAN I MAKE MY BEDROOM MORE COMFORTABLE?

☀ Soft, subdued colors create an intimate environment.

☀ Always have a bunch of fragrant and fresh flowers on a bedside table.

☀ Seductively drape a garland of silk flowers over lace or sheer curtains for a very romantic touch.

☀ Install a dimmer for the main light switch so you can keep the lights low, or buy a dimmer switch on an extension cord and attach it to your nightstand light.

☀ Fill the empty wall space behind the bed with draped fabric or curtains.

☀ The most interesting piece of furniture for a bedroom is an old-fashioned dressing table. Add a lace skirt and a glass top. Then display a framed mirror, perfume bottles, or a beautiful comb-and-brush set.

☀ Create your own instant storage space for rarely used items with a plastic garbage can and a round piece of wood. Use the garbage can as the base and the round piece of wood as the topper. Disguise the "table" by covering it with a floor-length round tablecloth.

☀ Small decorative curtain rods are a great place to hang scarves, belts, watches, and other small items.

☀ Be dramatic with paint. Use a special painting finish (refer to "Faux/Real" in chapter 3 for ideas). Paint also can disguise the size of the room. For example, if your bedroom is quite small, paint the walls a light color. Make the ceiling seem higher by painting it a lighter color than the walls.

☀ Wallpaper the bedroom ceiling. Select a soothing design as you'll be looking at it a lot when you're lying in bed.

☀ Because roller blinds (or shades) can make a room completely dark they are a good undertreatment for bedroom curtains. They also give privacy and offer a layer of insulation.

☀ If your bedroom window provides a wonderful view, arrange your bed so you can look out your window first thing in the morning.

☀ For a room with limited wall space, place the bed at an angle in one corner. Then make your bed the focal point of the room. Add a canopy, use a quilt as the main bedcover, and don't forget to pile on the pillows!

15 – Suite Dreams

❉ An interesting, yet inexpensive, headboard can be created by painting a horizontal rectangle on the wall where the bed will be placed. Frame the rectangle with decorative molding. Leave the painted area solid, apply a faux finish, or decorate with wallpaper cutouts or decals.

❉ Make a twin bed into a daybed by placing one long edge against a wall. Use two king-sized bed pillows along the wall and fill in empty spots with a collection of interesting throw pillows. (Refer to page 124 for ideas for making pillows from pillowcases.)

❉ Combine fabric and lace window treatments for eclectic charm.

❉ Use lace as a romantic canopy over a bed.

❉ A platform bed with drawers underneath and shelves in the headboard provides plenty of storage.

16 Someone's in the Kitchen

itchens are doing double duty in today's homes. It's not unusual for a kitchen to contain a home office or entertainment center as it continues to operate as a fast-food restaurant. Even though people are spending less time at home, that time is spent mainly in the kitchen. Here are some special ideas for this busy room and its neighbor, the dining room.

☀ Forgo a traditional window treatment made from fabric. Instead, hang an array of antique cooking utensils from a decorative rod. Your grandma's cupboard might be a good place to start looking.

☀ Cover inexpensive canisters with wallpaper (or coordinating wallpaper borders) to match your room exactly.

☀ Fill glass containers with lentils, pasta, and dried fruit for texture and color.

☀ Install some narrow shelves in the window and display a collection of interesting salt-and-pepper shakers.

☀ Drape dishtowels over a decorative rod to create a valance in the kitchen.

☀ Replace your plain kitchen knobs with colorful new ones.

☀ Install small cup hooks along a shelf edge and hang your collection of mugs from them.

16: – Someone's in the Kitchen

❀ Place mats and napkins don't have to match. Mix different shapes and colors on your table.

❀ Paint each kitchen chair a different color.

❀ On the other hand, a group of mismatched chairs seem cohesive if they are all stained or painted to match. Make matching chair cushions to coordinate the grouping.

❀ Increase storage space in kitchen cabinets by using lazy Susans and step-shelves.

❀ Store infrequently used items in places other than the kitchen.

❀ When selecting small appliances, consider the type that can be mounted underneath cabinets to free up counter space.

❀ Gather together multiples of old slate or chalkboards. Have the younger members of your family apply their artistic touch to the surface with chalk. Display the "art gallery" on the wall.

❀ Install a cork board inside a cabinet door for messages, shopping lists, or coupons.

☀ Use a coated wire grid and S hooks to hang mugs and utensils on the wall.

☀ Paint the inside of the most-used kitchen cupboard with a bold, upbeat color for a pleasant surprise to all who open it.

☀ Use a colander as a lampshade to create a luminaria-like light fixture. Drill a hole in the bottom of the colander to accommodate the electrical wiring. Purchase a hanging lamp kit and cover the wiring and cords that extend from the light to the ceiling with a gathered tube made from fabric that coordinates with the rest of the kitchen.

☀ Use tart pans with fluted edges as frames to hang on a wall.

☀ Window treatments used in the kitchen are likely to become stained and soiled. Select fabrics that are washable, shrink resistant, and colorfast.

☀ Paint the legs of an old card table a bright color and make a table cover to match.

☀ Create a sophisticated kitchen set by using inexpensive folding lawn chairs (buy them at summer's end for even more savings). Make a table base from plywood and use a plywood circle as a tabletop. No one will ever have to know that the table is not real—simply cover the table with a floor-length fabric table skirt.

☀ Use old water pitchers or antique teapots as containers for impromptu flower arrangements.

☀ Plant an herb window box in your kitchen. Good cooking herbs include parsley, rosemary, basil, oregano, marjoram, and dill. (See page 207 to make a tile-covered window box.)

☀ Use leftover fabric scraps to make coordinating place mats and napkins to complement your wallpaper and window treatments.

☀ Instead of traditional wallpaper, write your favorite recipes on the kitchen walls; use the many colorful markers available in craft stores (check the stenciling department). Add frames, stamps, and decals for added detail.

Dining Decor

Don't overlook the details when creating an exciting dining table for your family, friends, and guests to feast their eyes on!

☀ If you want to create a table full of romance, use lots of flowers, lace, and pastel colors. Mix flowered and solid-colored plates and use lacy napkins with a pastel table-cloth. Fill champagne flutes with flowers, and don't forget the candles!

☀ For a more contemporary look, use bright colors. Select brightly painted tableware (either solid or with a design) and glass and serving pieces in bold and unusual shapes. Add a colorful tablecloth and napkins. When serving beverages out of a pitcher, tie a napkin around the handle for extra punch.

☀ Use red, black, and white for a contemporary table presentation. Include geometric shapes in your table linens or even your plates. (They don't have to be round.)

☀ If you seldom eat in the dining room, a more casual approach to table decor may be to your liking. Cover the table with a denim tablecloth. Use pottery plates at each place setting and a colander filled with fresh flowers as a centerpiece (place flowers in a plastic container before placing in colander).

I LOVE TO ENTER-TAIN! HOW CAN I DECORATE MY TABLE FOR GUESTS?

⚉ For a sophisticated centerpiece, place mirrors under glass or crystal candlesticks.

⚉ Themed dinner parties are always fun to plan and attend. Why not treat your guests to a pasta dinner party? Look in your kitchen for table decoration ideas. Start with a centerpiece made from a loaf of bread. Scoop out the inside, place a plastic bowl in the scooped-out opening, and add a piece of floral foam. Then add flowers, pasta (spaghetti or other types), and fresh peppers. For a unique napkin ring, use a manicotti shell and pull the napkin through the opening. Place cards can be made from card stock with the names spelled with alphabet macaroni.

⚉ For an elegant table setting that glitters, use any one of the many popular metallic colors as a theme. Innovative dinner plates can be made easily with a stencil cut from adhesive-backed paper (Con-Tact brand is a familiar product). Place the stencil on the wrong side of a clear glass dinner plate. Spray the wrong side of the plate with metallic paint, remove the stencil, and you have instant elegance. Then, for more sparkle, use gold marking pens to decorate votive candle holders, paint the handles of your flatware, and decorate place cards.

⚉ Layer several sizes of tablecloths in coordinating colors at different angles for an interesting base for dinnerware.

⚉ Monogram table linens to personalize them in a very traditional way. This can easily be done using the preprogrammed embroidery features available on many sewing machines.

⚉ Appliqué a motif or design onto table linens. To appliqué by hand, fold under the raw edges of the motif 1/8 inch and whipstitch it in place. Or use the zigzag feature of your sewing machine. For an instant appliqué, use one of the popular fusible webs to adhere the motif to the table linen.

⚉ Fuse or stitch trim along the outside edges of napkins, table runners, and tablecloths.

16 – Someone's in the Kitchen

☀ Using textile paint, paint or stencil a design onto your table linens. This technique is also very effective with metallic paints.

☀ Use mismatched mittens as a silverware holder on cold wintry nights.

17 It's All in the Family Room

A family room is a place where family members can relax and be entertained. Here are some ways to make yours a place your whole family will love to spend time in.

⁕ Any warm color scheme is a good choice for this room. Grays are great if you add plenty of other accent colors.

⁕ Slipcovers are a cost-effective way to bring new life to aged and worn furniture. Alternative quick furniture coverups include a bed sheet, quilt, or even a tablecloth draped casually over the entire piece and tucked in.

⁕ Add a fabric throw for decoration and snuggling.

⁕ Add a mantel scarf to make a fireplace a colorful focal point. (See page 190 to learn how.)

⁕ For a relaxed, lived-in look, leave piles of books out on coffee tables, mantels, and in bookshelves.

⁕ Convert a birdcage into a planter. This container can be placed on a table or suspended from the ceiling.

⁕ An oversized ottoman serves both as a footrest and a coffee table. It is also an opportunity to introduce another color or pattern to the room.

⁕ Liven up oak flooring by installing black electrical tape in a geometric shape directly onto the floor. Pull up the tape when you move or want a change.

17 – It's All in the Family Room

☼ Old steamer trunks, pine crates, or even a concrete bird bath can be transformed into unique end tables.

☼ A worn pine floor is a perfect candidate for painted designs. Straight-line borders or geometric designs are good choices. Use latex paint, protected by coats of clear varnish or polyurethane.

☼ Revive a previously stained floor by stenciling designs on it in colors that complement the existing finish.

☼ Instead of painted floors, include area rugs in a room for just as much decorative impact.

☼ Frame old family photos and showcase them around the room or group them together on one table in different types of unusual frames. Or cover one wall with these framed photos.

☼ Keep in mind the proportion of a picture to the furniture if hung in close proximity. For example, a small picture will look lost next to a large piece of furniture.

☼ To include your artwork into the decorating scheme, connect it to other furnishings by hanging it 6 to 9 inches above furniture, or group several wall items together.

Decorating Child-Friendly Family Rooms

Family rooms are places for all members of the family to relax and be themselves. You want the youngest members of the family to feel welcome, too. To ensure this, consider the following suggestions to make yours a true family room.

※ Select durable allover floor covering for the family room such as no-wax vinyl or stain-resistant low-pile carpeting.

※ Have plenty of oversized pillows available to encourage use of the floor space. Cover pillows in sturdy fabric such as denim, canvas, or broadcloth.

※ For the walls, use a vinyl wallpaper or washable paint.

※ Select furniture that is simple in design, yet sturdy and easy to clean.

※ Include child-height storage shelves for games and toys.

※ A large table should be included in the room for art projects, crafts, and board games. Cover the floor underneath it with clear plastic so spills wipe up easily.

Decorating for Men

When decorating for the man in your home, consider his interests and personal preferences. Personal memorabilia is a great starting point when creating a room of distinction for a man.

MY HUSBAND DOESN'T WANT TO BE SURROUNDED BY FLOWERS. WHAT CAN I DO?

※ Special interests or hobbies may be the inspiration of a color scheme or theme. For example, if he is a fisherman, look for a wall border that incorporates tackle and the like into the design.

※ Most men like robust color combinations such as hunter green and tan, burgundy and navy, or autumn tones such as gold, terra cotta, and brown. Avoid pastels and florals.

※ Geometrics, plaids, tartans, checks, and stripes are usually good choices for a man's room.

※ Large-scaled patterns are better than small-scaled prints.

※ Sturdy fabrics such as wools, tweeds, corduroy, denim, suede, and leather add a masculine appeal to a room.

17 – It's All in the Family Room

❀ Select large, comfortable furniture pieces. Traditional furniture is always a favorite.

❀ Display leather-bound books and framed photos of activities that male members of your family enjoy.

❀ Fill assorted glass containers with nuts, bolts, and screws, or golf tees.

❀ If he collects baseball caps, hang them as a valance. (See page 200 for instructions.)

❀ Cover a basic frame with an old road map. To imitate aging, paint a gel stain over the surface.

18 Seasonal Decorating

hy would you want to decorate your home to correspond with the seasons? For the same reasons you change your wardrobe seasonally—for variety and to better enjoy the changing weather.

Quick-Change Decorating

Careful planning and a little ingenuity can result in quick-change decorating for special occasions, holidays, and the seasons.

☼ Don't overlook any places or spaces that can show off seasonal colors.

☼ A season's mood is set by color. A light, bright color palette conjures up thoughts of spring and summer. Warmer, richer hues from the color wheel bring to mind images of fall and winter.

☼ You don't need to refurbish your home completely to seasonally decorate. Slipcovers, fabric throws, decorative pillows, area rugs, and a few window treatment adaptations are all you need to change your decor.

☼ Purchase a chair or sofa that is already covered in a color from one season, i.e., white. This is a good color to work around for the summer months. In the fall, add a slipcover in dark, rich colors for a completely different look.

❀ Pillows are the easiest accent pieces to use to introduce the seasonal changes. Replace or recover pillows in the palette of the season.

❀ Accessories are the key to seasonal decorating. Try rotating artwork and a family photo collection. Change lamps and/or lampshades by borrowing from other rooms of your home.

❀ Create a seasonal collage of items that remind you of the seasons—a birdhouse, colorful plates, and fresh flowers for spring; richly colored leaves, pine cones, and gourds for fall and winter.

❀ Neutral-colored bedskirts and pillow shams can be used throughout the year. Make your bedcover reversible— spring and summer colors on one side, fall and winter colors on the other.

❀ The quickest way to change the feeling of a room is with scent. For spring and summer, select potpourri in a lilac or light floral fragrance; in winter, select a more woodsy or spicy smell.

Spring/Summer

After the long winter months, brighten up your world with a few easy changes.

❀ Smooth cotton and linen fabrics are perfect for spring and summer decorating. Use them to replace the flannel, velvet, or corduroy fabrics used in winter.

❀ Exchange your heavier window treatments with a café curtain or a valance. Select fabrics that are bright and cheery and that reflect the season. Valances are perfect window treatments for spring and summer because they expose more of the window to allow more light in and a chance to enjoy the scenery.

❀ If you have covered furniture with throws and table skirts, and windows with heavy draperies, remove them all to invite the openness of spring into your home.

❀ Use wispy sheers for spring and summer window treatments.

☀ Natural-textured throw rugs, such as sisal, add to the carefree attitude of summer.

☀ Add fresh bouquets of flowers everywhere.

☀ Remove wall decorations that look heavy (quilts, artwork) and replace them with mirrors to reflect the summer's sunshine.

☀ Fill the open area of an unused fireplace with fresh flowers in the spring and summer or paint a decorative fireplace screen and place it in front of the fireplace opening.

☀ Move your kitchen table and chairs close to a window so you can watch the arrival of spring in your garden.

☀ Create a more open environment in your home by storing some of the heavier pieces of furniture in the attic or basement. For example, remove a leaf from the dining room table and a piece from the sectional sofa to create the illusion of openness.

☀ Roll up area rugs and expose the hardwood floors.

☀ Replace some of your traditional pictures with botanical or fruit prints or brightly painted scenes of summer.

☀ Decorate your front door, foyer, banister, and mantel with grapevine branches, blossoming cherry blossoms, and potted tulips and hyacinths. A big straw hat and colorful streamers hung on the front door announce "welcome" to your guests.

☀ Bring some seasonal elements indoors by adding some lush, green plants, fresh flowers, and baskets of fruit around the room.

☀ Drape gauze casually over the headboard of your bed and over a curtain rod at a window for a summery feeling. Even the slightest breeze will cause the gauze to billow.

⚙ Keep tabletops uncluttered to give the room an airy feel.

⚙ In your bathroom, replace plush-pile scatter rugs with colorful cotton throw rugs.

Fall/Winter

When the leaves start falling from the trees and there is a nip in the air, we turn to our homes for cozy comfort. These ideas will help you enjoy the change to the cooler seasons.

⚙ Individual bowls of pine cones, leaves, nuts, or gourds placed around the house announce the arrival of fall.

⚙ Fuzzy wools, "snuggly" flannels, velvets, and corduroys are sure to fend off fall and winter chills.

⚙ Decorate your windows with layers of fabric. Start with a pull-down blind. Then add drapes at the sides of the windows and a valance over the top.

⚙ Arrange your furniture around your fireplace.

⚙ When selecting fabrics for winter, choose smooth and comfortable fabrics in rich colors; leave rough or nubby textures for spring.

⚙ Drape a velvet throw over a chair.

⚙ Replace small pillows with oversized pillows to make a room cozier.

⚙ Display your collection of dark-colored plates on a shelf.

⚙ Cover a wall with curtains in the bedroom. It will add warmth and comfort (as well as added insulation) during the coldest months.

⚙ Arrange a dark-colored patchwork quilt over a dining room table.

HOW CAN I BRING THE OUTSIDE IN TO ENJOY THE CHANGE OF SEASONS?

19 Helpful How-Tos

Here are complete instructions to help you with some of the do-it-yourself projects discussed in the previous chapters.

This How-To section begins with three techniques that are needed for most fabric projects. Following are fabric projects—for those who sew and those who don't. Finally, exciting painting projects and techniques will entice you to decorate walls, floors, and furniture once you see how easy they are.

You'll find a list of materials and step-by-step directions for the following types of projects:

- ✷ Window Treatments
- ✷ Fabric Accessories
- ✷ Wall Decor
- ✷ Floor Treatments
- ✷ Shelving
- ✷ Tile Projects
- ✷ Flowerpots

How To **Straighten Fabric**

You need to start all home decorating projects with fabric that has been straightened; that is, squared off across one end.

MATERIALS NEEDED • carpenter's square   • scissors
                  • fabric marker   • straight edge

DIRECTIONS

1. Work on a large, flat surface.

2. Unroll several yards of fabric, right side up. Bring the selvages together and fold the fabric so that it lies flat. For patterned fabric, make sure the motifs match exactly at the selvages. If the motifs don't match, you can manually straighten the fabric by pulling the whole width of fabric diagonally on the bias. (You need two people to do this.) Once the motifs match and the fabric lies flat, make a small snip with scissors in the selvage area (close to the cut edge) through both layers.

3. Unfold the fabric to a single thickness, right side up. At the snip marks, align the short blade of a carpenter's square with one selvage of the fabric (see figure). Using the other blade as a straight edge, draw a line across the fabric; begin at the snip. Continue this line across the width of the fabric. Ideally, the line will be at a perfect right angle to the selvage and the line will meet the snip at the opposite selvage edge. If there is a slight (1/2 inch or less) difference, follow the design in the fabric, rather than the drawn line.

4. Cut along the drawn line.

How To **Cut Fabric Lengths**

When working with decorator fabrics, it is important that each length of cut fabric be identical to the others. Not just the measurements, but also the design motifs need to be positioned at the same place. (Use materials listed above.)

DIRECTIONS

1. From the straightened end, measure and mark the cut length needed for your project along the selvage.

2. Using a straight edge, draw a line across the width of the fabric at this point. Before cutting, use a carpenter's square to see if the line is a perfect right angle with the selvage. Adjust the line if necessary (see above). Cut along this drawn line. This is the first, squared-off length.

3. To cut additional lengths, use the first length as a guide and place it directly on top of the remaining fabric; match motifs. Use a straight edge to mark this new cutting line (see figure).

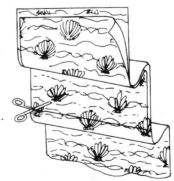

How To Match Repeats

Note: This information pertains only to 54-inch-wide decorator fabric.

What is a repeat? Patterned fabrics have motifs or designs that repeat uniformly. A "repeat" is the distance from an element on the motif to the same element on the next motif. The repeat distance will vary from pattern to pattern. Generally, the distance falls between 3 and 36 inches.

Along the selvage edge, the motifs will appear as if they were cut in half. However, if your eye travels directly across the width of the fabric you will find the other half of the motif. This is so when fabric widths need to be stitched together, the motifs will match exactly and the fabric will appear as if it is one long, continuous piece without any disruption of the design.

For professional-looking decorating accessories, the repeats should match at all seams. Avoid a center seam when piecing widths together. Generally, a full width of fabric is in the center of a project—a curtain, for example—with additional widths, or portions of widths, stitched to each side of the center.

MATERIALS NEEDED
- iron
- large ironing surface
- paper-backed fusible tape
- straight pins
- fabric scissors

DIRECTIONS

1. Lay the full width of the fabric right side up on a large work surface (preferably one you can iron on).

2. Lay additional panels along the appropriate side right side up. Press under the edges of adjoining panels toward the wrong side about 5/8 inch (fig. 1).

Figure 1

3. Fuse baste: Place a strip of paper-backed fusible tape, paper side up, close to the pressed edge of the adjoining fabric widths. Follow the manufacturer's instructions for iron temperature. Iron on the paper side, allow it to cool, and remove the paper. The heat transfers the adhesive to the fabric.

4. Lap the pressed seam allowance over the unpressed one, matching motifs exactly. Pin in place. Iron the two layers together; remove pins as you come to them to avoid making impressions in the fabric (fig. 2).

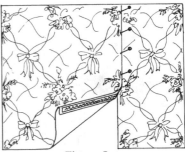

5. Arrange the fabric so the widths are right sides together and stitch directly in the crease line. Trim the seam allowance to 1/2 inch.

Figure 2

How To Make an Easy No-Sew Laced Blind

MATERIALS NEEDED
- canvas
- painted dowel rod
- eyelets
- paper-backed fusible hem tape
- coordinating cording (about four times the width of the blind)
- decorative rod, bracket, and finials

DIRECTIONS

1. Cut a piece of canvas 2 inches wider than the width of the window and 2 inches longer than the desired finished length of the shade.

2. Hem all the edges with a double 1/2-inch hem; use fusible hem tape or machine stitching to secure the hem in place.

3. Insert eyelets evenly spaced about 4 to 6 inches apart across the top and bottom edges of the shade.

4. Along the top edge, lace cording through the eyelets. First make a large single knot at one end of cord. Then, beginning at the outside corner of each panel, insert the cording through the first eyelet from front to back; pull the cord until the knot is against the eyelet. Bring the cording over the top edge to the front of the shade and insert it through the next eyelet. Continue lacing in this manner until all the eyelets are used. When all the eyelets are laced, make a large single knot at the end of the cord to secure it (see figure).

5. Insert the rod through the cording loops and hang the rod in brackets. Repeat the lacing process along the bottom edge. Insert a painted dowel or another decorative rod through the cording loops.

How To Make a Stagecoach Roller Shade

True to their functional origins, these blinds are a pretty and practical alternative to basic roller shades or miniblinds. This window treatment doesn't require much fabric, so it is very economical to construct.

MATERIALS NEEDED

- sewing machine
- contrasting fabric for ties
- 1-inch by 2-inch mounting board (cut to the measurement of the inside window width minus 1/2 inch)
- wooden dowel or cardboard tube, 1 1/2-inch diameter (cut to inside width measurement minus 1/2 inch)
- decorator and lining fabrics (lining will show when a shade is rolled; a shade can be self-lined or with a coordinating solid or print)
- staple gun
- two angle brackets

DIRECTIONS

Note: Use a 1/2-inch seam allowance unless otherwise noted.

1. Measure the inside width and length of the window.

2. Cut decorator and lining fabrics into rectangles that are equal to the width of the window plus 1 inch and the length of the window plus 4 inches.

3. From the contrasting fabric, cut eight strips 3 inches wide by the length of the window plus 12 inches.

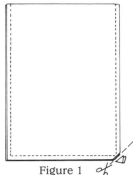

4. Place the decorator fabric and lining right sides together. Stitch along three sides; leave the top edge open for turning. Clip the corners of the seam allowances diagonally and turn the shade right side out (fig. 1). Press the shade smooth and flat; arrange the shade so that the lining and decorator fabrics are equally divided and neither shows on the opposite side. Clean-finish the open edges together with a zigzag or overcast stitch.

Figure 1

5. Stitch two tie strips right sides together along three sides; leave one short end open. Clip the corners and turn right side out. Press smooth. Make the remaining three ties. Clean-finish the open edges together with a zigzag or overcast stitch.

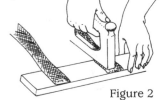

6. Cover the mounting board with shade fabric by wrapping it like a package with fabric and stapling the fabric in place. Trim excess fabric at the corners so they are smooth and tight.

7. Cover the ends of the dowel or cardboard tube with shade fabric; use a hot glue gun and a large fabric circle.

Figure 2

8. Position a tie about 4 inches from each end on the right side of the mounting board; staple to secure (fig. 2).

9. Center the shade on top of the right side of the mounting board; the top edge of the shade should be even with the back edge of board and the decorator fabric is face up. Staple the shade to the board every inch or so to hold the blind securely in place.

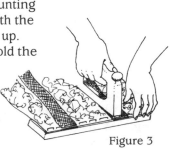

10. Staple the remaining two ties over the shade, lining them up with the first ties (fig. 3).

11. Place the shade on your worktable right side up. Staple the bottom edge of the shade to the dowel. Roll the dowel to the desired length and use fabric ties to hold it in place.

Figure 3

12. Attach the blind to the inside of the window frame using angle brackets.

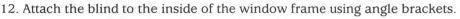

How To Embellish Sheer Curtains with Ribbons

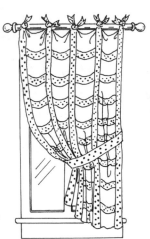

Use inexpensive, sheer, ready-made curtains and yards of beautiful ribbon to create a one-of-a-kind window treatment that requires very little sewing.

MATERIALS NEEDED
- ready-made sheer curtains
- erasable fabric marker
- paper-backed fusible tape
- decorative rod, finials, and brackets
- ribbon to match your decor

DIRECTIONS

1. Plan your ribbon design on paper to determine how much ribbon you will need for your creation. Ribbons can be placed vertically or horizontally over the surface of the curtain.

2. Along the top edge, determine the placement of ribbon ties; the first and last set of ties should be as close to each side edge as possible. The remaining sets of ties should be evenly spaced 6 to 8 inches apart. For a more dramatic look, space the ties even farther apart for more "droop" between the ties. When calculating ribbon yardage, add 20 inches for each planned tie.

3. Cut the ribbon for the ribboned surface design into desired lengths plus 1 inch. Apply paper-backed fusible tape to the wrong side of the ribbon; follow the manufacturer's instructions.

4. Mark guidelines on the curtain front and fuse the ribbon over them. Turn under the ends of the ribbon 1/2 inch for a clean finish.

5. Cut ties from the ribbon. Fold each tie in half. Place the folded edge of a ribbon tie on the wrong side of the curtain along the top edge and stitch it in place to secure.

6. Tie the ribbons evenly over the rod. Insert the rod in its brackets and arrange the curtains into pleasing folds.

How To Make a No-Sew Valance

MATERIALS NEEDED
- 54-inch-wide fabric, 1 1/4 yards
- paper-backed fusible tape
- decorator rod, finials, and brackets

DIRECTIONS

1. Fold 54-inch-wide fabric in half crosswise (the selvages should meet along each side edge) to form an 18-by-54-inch rectangle.

2. Overlap and fuse the cut ends together to form a tube (see figure).

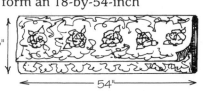

18"

54"

3. Insert a decorative rod through the finished tube and hang.

4. Arrange the fabric into luscious folds; tuck the printed selvages under so they can't be seen. Note: One yard of fabric will cover a 36-inch-wide window at a fullness 1 1/2 times the width of the window. If the window is wider, add additional fabric tubes.

How To Make Curtains From Dishtowels

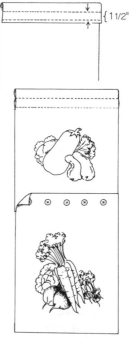

MATERIALS NEEDED
- at least two napkins or dishtowels per panel
- coordinating buttons
- decorative rod, brackets, and finials

DIRECTIONS

1. For the rod pocket, fold over and press 3 inches toward the wrong side along the top edge. Stitch the pocket along the finished edge.

2. Then stitch another, parallel row of stitching 1 1/2 inches from the first. These two stitching lines will form a channel in which the rod is inserted.

3. Three inches up from the bottom edge of this napkin or dishtowel overlap a second napkin or dishtowel. Handstitch evenly spaced buttons along the top edge of the second napkin or dishtowel to secure the two together. Add more napkins or towels in the same manner to reach desired length.

How To Plan Your Tiebacks

Tiebacks are truly one of the most economical accents you can make for your home! Depending on the style, most tiebacks require very little fabric. Plain curtains become more attention getting by the addition or replacement of existing tiebacks.

DIRECTIONS

1. Cut a strip of scrap fabric that is 4 inches wide and 30 inches long. Use this strip to determine the best tieback length for your curtains or drapes.

2. Wrap the strip around the curtain where you want the tieback and arrange the curtain into attractive folds and/or curves. Secure it in place temporarily with pins and stand back to see if you like what you see. Adjust if necessary.

3. While the strip is still in place, make a small pencil mark on the wall where a cup hook will be installed.

4. Remove the strip and measure it to determine the finished length you need.

How To Make Mini-Jabot and Rosette Tiebacks

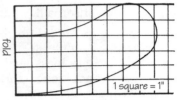

Figure 1

MATERIALS NEEDED

- two cup hooks
- removable fabric marker
- coordinating fabric for tieback and mini-jabot, 7/8 yard
- decorator fabric for tieback and mini-jabot, 7/8 yard
- fusible interfacing, 1/2 yard
- gridded pattern tracing cloth, 3/4 yard
- four brass or plastic rings, each 5/8 inch across

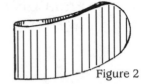

Figure 2

DIRECTIONS

1. Transfer the tieback pattern onto a gridded pattern tracing cloth; adjust the length as needed along the fold (fig. 1). Using the pattern you just drafted, cut two tieback shapes each from decorator and lining fabrics and fusible interfacing. Trim 1/2 inch from all edges of the interfacing piece.

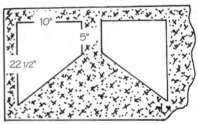

Figure 3

2. Center the interfacing on the wrong side of the lining and fuse. Place the decorator and lining tieback shapes with right sides together. Stitch around all sides; leave an opening for turning along one long edge.

3. Trim the seam allowances to 1/4 inch to eliminate bulk. Turn tiebacks right side out. Press smooth. Turn under the edges of the opening and stitch or fuse it closed. Handstitch rings to tieback ends (fig. 2).

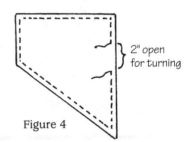

2" open for turning

Figure 4

4. Refer to the diagram (fig. 3) and draw two jabot shapes onto the wrong side of the decorator and lining fabrics; use measurements (10 inches, 5 inches and 12 1/2 inches) as indicated. Cut out jabots.

5. Place mini-jabot fabrics right sides together. Stitch as shown in the diagram (fig. 4); leave a 2-inch opening for turning. Clip corners diagonally and turn right side out. Press smooth. Handstitch the opening closed.

6. Starting at the inside edge of the jabot, fold it into staggered-width, accordion-style pleats until the top of the jabot measures 3 inches. Steam press to set folds (fig. 5).

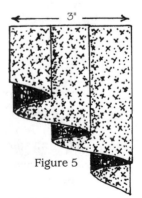

3"

Figure 5

7. Refer to the finished diagram and place a jabot under the end of each tieback. Handstitch in place. Place a rosette over it and stitch in place.

How To Make a Fabric Rosette

You'll find many places to use this fun decorating embellishment.

MATERIALS NEEDED
- fabric for rosette, 1/4 yard
- sewing machine with zigzag capabilities
- silk cording for gathering
- fabric glue

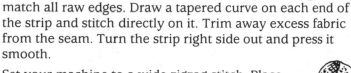

Figure 1

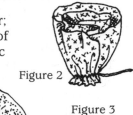

Figure 2

Figure 3

DIRECTIONS

1. For each rosette, cut a strip from your fabric, 4 1/2 inches long and the width of the fabric. Also cut a circle 2 inches in diameter. Fold the strip in half lengthwise with the wrong sides together; match all raw edges. Draw a tapered curve on each end of the strip and stitch directly on it. Trim away excess fabric from the seam. Turn the strip right side out and press it smooth.

2. Set your machine to a wide zigzag stitch. Place gathering cord 3/8 inch from the raw edge of the strip. Stitch over the cord, being careful not to catch it in the stitching. Gather the strip by pulling on the cord until the gathers are tight (fig. 1).

3. Beginning at one end, roll the strip tightly twice to form the center of the rose. Then form the rest of the rose by rolling more loosely the strip around the center (fig. 2). Glue or stitch the base of the rosette to secure its shape. Glue the fabric circle over the raw edges of the rosette (fig. 3).

How To Make No-Sew Braided Tiebacks

MATERIALS NEEDED
- paper-backed fusible tape
- two cup hooks
- three coordinating fabrics, 1/4 yard each
- 3/4-inch diameter uncovered cording, 6 yards
- four brass or plastic rings, each 5/8 inch

DIRECTIONS

Note: These directions will yield two tiebacks, each 24 inches long. If you need a different size, reduce or enlarge the cut length of the cord in a 2:3 ratio to the finished length of the tieback. For example, for a 20-inch tieback, the cut cord length is 30 inches.

1. Cut cording into six equal lengths.

2. Cut two strips from each fabric, each 3 by 38 inches.

3. Place a fabric strip wrong side up on your work surface. Along one long edge, fold and press ¹/4 inch to the wrong side. Directly on top of fold, apply the paper-backed fusible tape. Along opposite unfinished edge, apply fusible tape. When cool, remove paper backing from both sides (fig. 1).

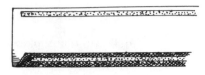

Figure 1

4. Place the cording in the center of a fabric strip. Fabric should extend 1 inch beyond the top and bottom ends of the cord (fig. 2). Wrap the unfinished edge of the strip around the cord and fuse it to the cord. Then wrap the folded edge around to cover the raw edge and fuse (fig. 3).

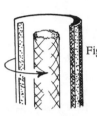

Figure 2

Figure 3

5. Tuck the ends of the fabric in and whipstitch them closed.

6. Tack three cords together (one from each fabric) with a few handstiches. Plait the three cords the entire length. When finished, tack the three cords together at the other end (fig 4).

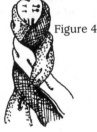

Figure 4

Figure 5

7. Sew a brass or plastic ring on the wrong side of each end of the tieback to finish (fig. 5).

How To Make an Easy, Reversible Duvet Cover

Duvets are feather- or batting-filled quilted comforters and a very popular bedcovering worldwide. Duvet covers are very versatile—especially if they are made to be reversible for quick-change decorating. Stitching a duvet cover is little more than making an oversized pillowcase. This project is a great way to use sheets in your decorating plan—especially if you are going to launder the cover frequently.

MATERIALS NEEDED
- two different fabrics or sheets, one for each side of a duvet cover
- ribbon for ties, 3¹/2 yards
- measuring tools
- twill tape for corner anchors
- sewing machine

DIRECTIONS

Note: Use ¹/2-inch seam allowance unless otherwise noted.

1. Spread the duvet to be covered on the floor and take accurate measurements. Add the depth of the comforter plus 1 inch to both the length and width measurements. These are your cutting dimensions. If you're using sheets, select a sheet that is large enough to accommodate these measurements. If you're using fabric, more than likely you will have to piece fabric together to obtain these measurements. Determine the number of lengths needed, plus additional fabric to match the motifs at each seam and ⁵/8 yard for the facing. You do not have to face a sheet because it is already hemmed.

Figure 1

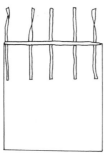

Figure 2

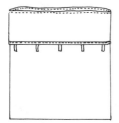

Figure 3

2. If you need to stitch fabric together to obtain needed size, cut one width in half lengthwise and stitch one half width to each side of the full width (fig. 1).

3. From sheets or fabric, cut two rectangles to the cutting dimensions in step 1. For the facing, cut two strips, each 10 inches by the comforter's cutting-width measurement.

4. Cut the twill tape into four lengths, each 15 inches. Place one tie at each bottom corner. These are the corner anchors. Set aside the remaining two.

5. Place the cover fabrics right sides together. Stitch down both long sides and across one short (bottom) end (fig. 2). Reinforce the corners by stitching again directly over the previous stitching. Clip corners diagonally to eliminate bulk. Finish the seam with a zigzag or overcast stitch. Turn the cover right side out and press it smooth.

6. Cut the ribbon for ties into ten equal lengths, each 12 inches. Equally space the ties in pairs across both sides of the open end of the cover. Make sure ties are aligned on the front and back (fig. 3). If making your cover from sheets, stitch ties to cover now. Then proceed to step 10.

7. Stitch the facing strips together end to end to form one large circle. Press these seams open. Along one edge, fold under and press a double 1/2-inch hem. Stitch along the folded edge.

8. Place the facing right sides together along the open edge of the cover; match raw edges and side seams. Stitch the facing to the cover through all layers (including the ribbon ties) (fig. 4). Press this seam open.

9. Turn the facing to the inside of the cover; press. Secure the facing in place by either stitching around the opening of the comforter through all layers or with paper-backed fusible webbing.

10. Stitch the remaining twill-tape anchor ties to each corner of the bottom edge of the duvet. Insert duvet into comforter. Tie the ties together at each corner so comforter stays in place.

How To Make the Easiest Pillow in the World

This easy pillow needs only a few stitches. Make up several in coordinating colors and display them together.

MATERIALS NEEDED
(finished size:
16 inches square)

- 16-inch pillow form
- sewing machine
- decorator fabric (38 by 17 inches)
- thread
- tape measure
- scissors

DIRECTIONS

1. Cut a rectangle 38 inches by 17 inches.

2. Along each short end, fold under and press a double 1-inch hem. Stitch along the fold line (fig. 1).

3. Arrange the fabric with right sides together so they overlap in the back as shown and the piece measures 17 inches square. Pin layers together (fig. 2).

4. Stitch top and bottom edges with a 1/2-inch seam allowance. Clip corners diagonally to eliminate bulk (fig. 3). Turn the cover right side out. Insert a pillow form through the opening.

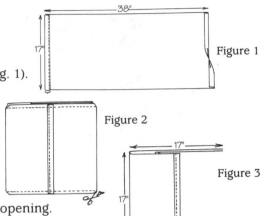

Figure 1

Figure 2

Figure 3

How To Cover a Lampshade with Fabric

Fabric-covered lampshades are quick and easy to make. While you are in a creative mood, consider decorating the base of the lamp to coordinate with your shade. Once you see how easy it is to refresh and update a lampshade, you'll want to redo all of the shades in your home.

MATERIALS NEEDED
- lampshade
- fabric
- optional: trim for embellishment
- scissors
- fabric glue

DIRECTIONS

1. To draft the shape of your lampshade, place the shade onto a large sheet of tissue paper. Roll the shade, marking the top and bottom edges as you go. Add 1 inch to all edges for finishing allowance (fig. 1).

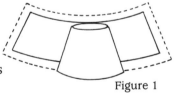

Figure 1

2. Carefully cut out the shade pattern. Test the fit on your shade; make any adjustments needed. From this paper pattern, determine the amount of fabric you need. Take the pattern with you to the fabric store and use it as a guide.

3. Once you've cut the pattern from the fabric, press under 1/2 inch toward the wrong side along one edge. Lay fabric arc on a large, flat surface. Place the shade on the middle of the arc. Carefully arrange the fabric arc around the shade, beginning at one side. Glue unfinished edge to shade (fig. 2).

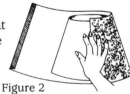

Figure 2

4. When the arc is arranged around the shade, overlap the finished edge over the unfinished edge for a neat appearance; trim excess fabric away. Glue the finished edge in place with fabric glue (fig. 3).

5. Trim the top and bottom edges to 1/2 inch. So that the upper edge will fit smoothly, make vertical cuts every 1/2 inch or so to within 1/8 inch of the shade frame. Apply fabric glue to the wrong side of the shade along the upper and lower edges.

Figure 3

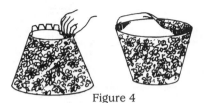

Figure 4

6. Fold the fabric smoothly over the edge of the shade and hold it in place for several seconds to let the glue bond. Make sure there are no tucks along the edges (fig. 4).

Design Option:

Adding purchased trim to the bottom and/or top edges is a quick, easy, and attractive way to embellish your shade.

Trims come in a variety of textures including woven braid, tassel fringe, ball fringe, and cording. Apply the trim 3 to 4 inches at a time, using fabric glue. Always begin and end trim at the center back seam of the shade.

How To Install Gathered-Lace Wall Panels

MATERIALS NEEDED
- voile, lace, or netting
- ribbon to match fabric
- molding
- tape measure
- scissors
- staple gun
- fabric glue

DIRECTIONS

1. Paint and install molding at the desired height along the wall.

2. Measure the distance between the bottom edge of the molding and the top of the baseboard. To this measurement, add two inches. This is the cut length of each lace panel. The cut width of each lace panel is 20 inches.

3. Determine the number of lace panels needed. (The finished width of the panels is 10 inches.) Cut as many lace pieces as necessary. Mark the finished width of each panel lightly on the wall below the molding and in corresponding positions along the baseboard.

4. Turn under 1/2 inch along the top edge of each panel. Staple the fabric directly underneath the molding strip; pleat as you go to gather the fabric to fit between the finished width markings. Repeat with the bottom edge of the panel in the same manner.

5. Gather the center of each panel together and secure it with a length of ribbon tied into a bow.

6. Optional: Cover the staples with a length of ribbon or cording glued in place.

How To Cover Walls with Fabric

Here are two of the easiest ways to cover your walls with fabric. Fabric-covered walls add warmth to any room and can, of course, match other fabric used in the room. The main advantage of using fabric over wallpaper is that you can easily remove the fabric from the walls and reuse it, making fabric a better decorating option for a college dorm room or an apartment.

19 - Helpful How-Tos

Method 1: Starching

For best results, use this method on smooth, light-colored walls that have no visible cracks.

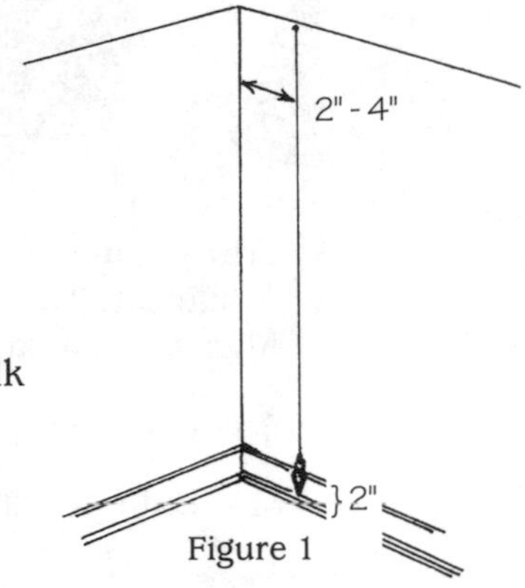

MATERIALS NEEDED
- decorator fabric
- measuring tape
- liquid starch
- metal straight edge
- large container for starch
- string, plumb line, plumb bob, and chalk
- plastic sheets or drop cloth
- wide paintbrush
- tacks
- utility knife

2" - 4"

}2"

Figure 1

DIRECTIONS

1. Paint all trim, moldings, and windows before beginning. Also remove switch plates, vent covers, and any curtain hardware. Clean the walls with a mild detergent if they are painted, or vacuum them if they are covered with wallpaper. Make sure new walls are primed with paint before covering them with fabric.

2. "Plumb" the wall as if you were applying wallpaper. The plumb line is the true vertical line of each wall and should be positioned about 2 to 4 inches in from the corner (fig. 1). This line will act as a guideline so the fabric panels will hang perfectly straight. To create a plumb line, tie a plumb bob to one end of the string and the other end to a tack. Rub the string with carpenter's chalk. Hang the string from the ceiling line (where the wall and ceiling meet) with the tack and when the plumb bob stops swinging, make a mark on the wall about 2 inches above the baseboard. Hold the string taut just above the weight with one hand and use the other hand to snap the string against the wall. This will leave a chalk line. Repeat this process on every wall you are going to cover.

3. Measure the wall you want to cover from floor to ceiling and corner to corner to help determine the amount of fabric you will need to cover the wall(s). Decorator fabric is usually 54 inches wide. Plan on matching the pattern repeats. Add one repeat measurement—the distance between the motifs of a fabric's pattern—for every width of fabric you need. For example, add 18 inches of fabric if the repeat of your fabric is 6 inches and you need three widths of fabric to cover the wall.

4. Cut the fabric into lengths that are the floor-to-ceiling measurement plus 6 inches to allow for potential unevenness in the ceiling line. After the first length of fabric is cut, use this panel as a guide and cut subsequent panels exactly the same; match repeats if necessary. Remove the selvages from the edges of the fabric. On the wrong side of the fabric, mark a T at the top edge.

5. Apply a generous coat of starch to the wall surface with the paintbrush. Also apply a thin coat to the wrong side of the fabric.

baseboard

Figure 2

trim away

Figure 3

6. Begin applying the fabric to the wall. Align the edge with the plumb line and allow 3 inches to extend beyond the top and bottom. If you are covering more than one wall, allow the first fabric panel to wrap into the starting corner for 2 to 4 inches (fig. 2). Smooth the fabric with the palm of your hands, being sure not to stretch the fabric. Apply additional starch to the wall and/or fabric as needed.

7. Continue adding fabric panels; match the design motifs in the fabric at the "seams." This may involve overlapping the fabric edges slightly.

8. Once dry, trim the fabric evenly along the top and bottom edges with a very sharp utility knife and a straight edge (fig. 3). Also, trim away the overlap as follows: Hold the straight edge vertically against the wall and with a utility knife, slash through both layers. Remove the fabric strip from the overlapping edge. Then remove the underlapping strip by pulling back the fabric gently. Rearrange so fabric butts together and reseal by applying starch to the seam.

9. Should air bubbles occur, prick them with a pin and smooth the fabric against the wall.

Method 2: Shirring

This technique requires more fabric than the starching method, but it creates a very luxurious look in a room. Structural faults and deteriorated walls are well hidden among the many folds of fabric. For best results, use light- to medium-weight fabric.

For a money-saving option, use cardboard tubes discarded from carpet and fabric stores as rods. To hang this type of "rod," insert a length of strong cord through the tube opening and tie it onto cup hooks that are installed at ceiling height

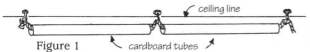

ceiling line

Figure 1   cardboard tubes

(fig. 1). If you select this option, add additional fabric to accommodate the girth of the tube. Measure the tube's circumference and add 1 inch. Add this number to the 6 inches suggested in the following instructions. You will also have to adjust the rod pocket stitching lines to accommodate the cardboard tubes.

MATERIALS NEEDED
- decorator fabric
- measuring tape
- sewing machine
- screwdriver
- narrow curtain rods with brackets (or cardboard tubes)
- power drill
- screws
- thread

DIRECTIONS

1. To calculate fabric yardage, measure the width of the wall(s) to be covered. You'll need 2½ to 3 times this measurement for necessary fullness; generally, lightweight fabrics look better with more fullness. Divide this multiple by the width of fabric to find how many fabric widths you will need for adequate coverage. To determine the cut length, add 12 inches for top and bottom rod

pockets to the wall-height measurement, or add 6 inches for a top rod pocket and 8 inches for a double 4-inch bottom hem (the fabric will hang loosely at the bottom). Multiply the number of widths needed by the cut length for the total yardage needed. Add an allowance for matching the designs (approximately one repeat distance for every width of fabric).

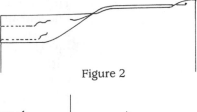

Figure 2

2. Cut fabric to determined lengths. Along the top edge of each fabric width, fold under 3 inches on the wrong side and press. Then turn the raw edge under 1/2 inch and press. Stitch close to this fold line. Stitch another row approximately 1 1/2 inches from the first (fig. 2). Repeat along the bottom edge if you are using another rod pocket along the floor. If you are hemming the curtains, fold over and press 8 inches to the wrong side. Then tuck under 4 inches to meet the pressed fold line for the bottom hem (fig. 3).

Figure 3

3. Locate the wall studs and mount the hardware brackets about 1 1/4 inches down from the ceiling and, for the bottom rod pocket, 1 1/2 inches up from the floor (or wherever the curtains will end).

4. Insert the rod through the top rod pocket of each fabric panel and mount it onto the brackets. Repeat for the lower edge. Adjust gathers; make sure the printed selvage is hidden among the folds. Note: There should be some tension in the fabric between the top and bottom rods, but not enough that the rods bow in the center. You may need to add some support brackets in the center of the rod to support the weight of the fabric.

How To Make a Fabric-Covered Room Divider

Divide your rooms and conquer decorating dilemmas with this versatile accessory.

MATERIALS NEEDED
- four wood panels, 6 feet by 12 inches by 1 inch
- six folding screen hinges
- decorator fabric, 2 yards
- batting
- staple gun and staples
- latex paint to match fabric
- 19 yards ribbon, 3/4 inch wide
- fabric glue
- sandpaper
- tack cloth
- primer
- paintbrush
- scissors

Note: If the fabric you select has a large design, you must add additional yardage so all the panels will match.

DIRECTIONS

1. Prepare wooden panels for painting (on one side only) by sanding the surface smooth. Remove dust with a tack cloth. Paint with primer and allow it to dry completely. Sand the panel again to ensure the surface is smooth. Apply paint in a color that will coordinate with your fabric. Allow it to dry. Apply a second coat if necessary.

Figure 1

Figure 2

2. Cut four batting panels the exact size of the panel. Cut four fabric panels the size of each panel plus 3/4 inch on each edge.

3. Place batting on the unpainted side of the wooden panels. Trim it if necessary for a perfect fit.

4. Center the fabric right side up on the batting-covered side of the wooden panel.

5. Staple the edge of the fabric to the sides of the wooden panel (fig. 1). Begin by stapling once in the center of one long side, then directly opposite the first staple on the other long side. Repeat the process at each end. Then fill in the sides with staples until the fabric is smoothly applied. If needed, trim excess fabric so edges don't extend beyond edges of the board.

6. Glue ribbon around the perimeter of each wooden panel on all edges to conceal staples (fig. 2).

7. Mark hinge placement on the edges of the panel about 4 inches from each short end and in the middle of each panel. Install hinges according to package instructions.

How To "Slipcover" a Folding Screen

Use these directions to construct a fireplace screen or a full-length screen to use in a corner or as a room divider. The fabric "slipcovers" can be changed throughout the year to accommodate seasons and special holidays since each panel is slipcovered separately.

MATERIALS NEEDED

- drill
- fabric
- shelving, 12 inches wide
- folding screen hinges: six for a fireplace screen; eight for a full-size screen. The hinges should be no wider than the edge of the shelving.
- screwdriver
- thread
- sewing machine

DIRECTIONS
Folding Screen

1. Cut the shelving to appropriate lengths. You can cut the shelving yourself or have it cut for you at a home center. If you are making a fireplace screen, measure the height of the opening of your fireplace and add 2 inches (the total will be about 30 inches). For a floor-length screen, the shelving should be approximately 60 inches long.

2. Attach hinges to the side edges of the boards. Drill a hole first with a drill bit that is slightly smaller than the screw you are using. For a fireplace screen, attach the hinges about 4 inches from each end. For a full-length screen, place the hinges about 4 inches from each end and in the center of each board.

Slipcovers

1. To determine the amount of fabric needed for your screen, measure the width of the screen panel and add 2 inches for side hems. This is the cut width of the fabric. Then measure the length and thickness of the panel, multiply by 2, and add 1 1/2 inches for ease and seam allowances. This is the cut length. Purchase enough fabric for four pieces cut to these measurements. If necessary, add additional fabric for matching repeats.

2. From fabric, cut four panels to the cut length and width measurements in step 1.

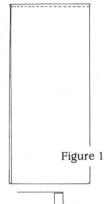

Figure 1

3. With right sides together, stitch the short ends of each slipcover panel together with a 1/2-inch seam allowance (fig. 1). Press each seam open.

4. To form side hems, fold 1/2 inch to the wrong side of each long edge of the panel and press the fold. Then fold 1/2 inch under again and press (fig. 2). Stitch the hem along the folded edge. Turn the slipcovers right side out and arrange them so the seam is at the bottom of each panel.

5. Ties can be made from 15-inch lengths of coordinating fabric, ribbon, or cording. For a fireplace screen, you will need 18 ties; for a full-size screen, you will need 24 ties. The more ties you include, the fewer gaps will occur between the slipcover panels.

6. If making fabric ties, cut two strips of fabric, each 4 by 15 inches. Press 1/2 inch on the short ends of each strip toward the wrong side of fabric (fig. 3). Then arrange the strip so the raw edges meet in the center; press. Then fold the strip in half lengthwise and press. Topstitch across the short ends and along the open long edge (fig. 4).

7. Mark placement for ties where desired on each side of the slipcovers. Stitch the ties in pairs along both edges of the panels.

8. Slip one slipcover over screen; slide it to the center panel. Slip the remaining covers over the end panels of the screen. Tie the ties together along all edges to hold the slipcover in place.

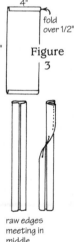

— 1/2"

Figure 2

1/2"

4"

fold over 1/2"

15"

Figure 3

Figure 4

raw edges meeting in middle

How To Make a Mantel Scarf

This accessory will warm up any mantel. Make several to go with the seasons and holidays throughout the year!

MATERIALS NEEDED
- sewing machine
- decorator fabric and lining
- flat braid or trim to coordinate with fabric
- scissors
- optional: tassels

DIRECTIONS

1. Measure the length (from side to side) and depth (from front to back) of the top of the mantel. Determine how long a drop you want over the front of the mantel and add it to the depth measurement. To the length and depth

measurements, add 1 inch for seam allowance. From both the decorator and lining fabrics, cut a rectangle to these dimensions.

2. Determine the design you want along the drop edge. Draft this design along one long edge of the cut rectangle and cut along this line.

3. Place the decorator fabric and lining pieces right sides together. Stitch around all edges, leaving an opening along the back edge for turning.

4. Clip all corners diagonally to remove bulk. Turn the mantel cover right side out and press smooth. Handstitch the opening closed.

5. Pin flat braid around all edges of the mantel cover, and carefully machine stitch it to the cover.

How To Make a Felt-Covered Board

These colorful and functional boards can set the mood or theme of your child's room. Make more than one, using different colors.

MATERIALS NEEDED
- homasote board (cut to desired size)
- felt to cover the board
- assorted felt pieces for letters, numbers, and shapes
- staple gun
- measuring tools
- scissors
- wall anchors

DIRECTIONS

1. Cut the homasote board to the desired size. Cut a piece of felt large enough to cover the entire surface plus 6 inches added to both the length and the width.

2. Center the felt over the board; wrap the excess to the back and staple it in place. Make sure the felt fits tightly over the board. Miter the corners for a neat finish.

3. From assorted felt pieces, cut out large letters, numbers, and shapes. Use a coloring book or computer-generated images for the patterns.

4. Hang the board at child's height for easy access.

How To Stencil with Lace on Fabric

Consider the possibilities—pillows, valances, table skirts and toppers, even duvet covers. You can stencil anything—from plain cotton fabric to ready-made curtains and valances.

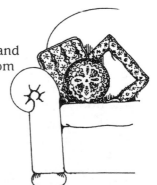

MATERIALS NEEDED
- fabric or ready-made accessory
- masking tape
- lace (plastic or crocheted)
- spray paint (textile or latex paint)

DIRECTIONS

1. Lace comes in a variety of textures. Select a lace with a well-defined pattern. Plastic "crocheted" tablecloths are often good sources of lace designs. They work well because the tablecloths can accommodate various-sized projects.

2. Refer to the manufacturer's instructions to prepare the fabric to receive the paint.

3. Tape the fabric securely to a large work surface. Select the area of the lace that you want reproduced and lay it on top of the fabric. Tape the lace to your work surface to secure.

4. Spray paint onto the fabric; paint will go through the lace to create the design. Allow the paint to dry and then remove the lace stencil.

5. Refer to the manufacturer's instructions to set the paint into the fabric.

How To Paint a Floorcloth

Paint a canvas floorcloth as an alternative to a plain wood floor or an area rug.

MATERIALS NEEDED
- press cloth
- clear acrylic varnish
- heavy-grade artist's canvas (available at art supply stores)
- fusible bonding web (such as Stitch Witchery), 3/4 inches wide
- acrylic or latex paints in assorted colors
- assorted paintbrushes or sponges
- T-square, yardstick, or ruler
- optional: precut stencils
- gesso primer
- pencil

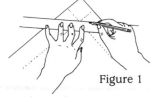

Figure 1

DIRECTIONS

1. Measure the area to be covered by the floorcloth; add 2 inches all around for the hem.

2. Along each edge, mark a 1-inch hem. At each corner, draw a diagonal line to form a triangle (fig. 1). Trim the triangle away with a scissors.

3. Press under hem along all edges. The mitered corners should line up perfectly (fig. 2). Place the fusible web between the hem and the wrong side of the floorcloth. Cover the area with a damp press cloth and with an iron set on medium heat, steam press for 10 seconds. Lift and move the iron to another section—do not slide the iron. Repeat until the entire hem is fused in place.

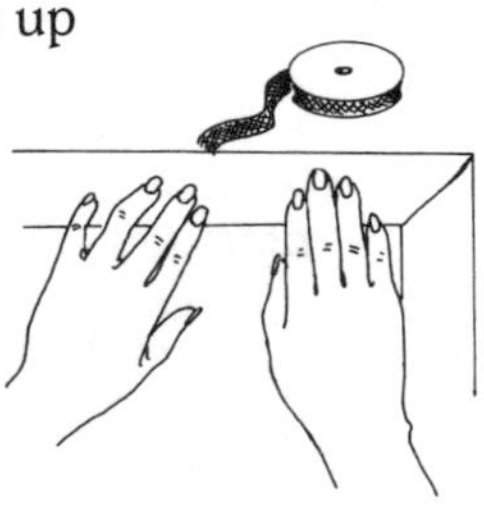

4. Apply one coat of gesso over the entire surface of the right side of the floorcloth. Allow it to dry thoroughly before continuing.

Figure 2

5. Draw your design on the floorcloth with a pencil. Note: If you are going to paint the design freehand or use precut stencils,

you do not have to do this step. Use a ruler, yardstick, or T-square to draw grids or straight lines.

6. Paint the design onto the floorcloth as desired.

7. Allow the floorcloth to dry completely, then brush on a coat of clear acrylic varnish to seal the paint and stiffen the cloth. Repeat the process at least three times; allow each coat to dry thoroughly before the next coat is applied.

How To Make a Stencil from Fabric or Wallpaper

Use this technique to re-create a favorite design found in wallpaper, fabric, china, or even a tablecloth in stencil form. Use this stencil on furniture or on a wall as a creative border.

MATERIALS NEEDED
- fabric or wallpaper design
- stencil plastic sheet
- sharp craft knife
- protective cutting surface

DIRECTIONS

1. Select a motif from the fabric or wallpaper to create a stencil from.

2. Photocopy the motif on a black-and-white copier.

3. If necessary, enlarge or reduce the motif until it is an appropriate size for the area you are covering. Trace the design on the template plastic.

4. Using a sharp craft knife and a protective cutting surface, carefully cut around the design. Cut out all the shapes that will use the same color of stencil paint from the same piece of plastic; shapes that will use additional colors of paint require their own stencils.

5. Apply paint to a stenciling brush, wipe off excess paint, and begin to stencil opened areas.

How To Paint Plaid Design on Walls, Fabric, or Furniture

This easy technique can be used on both furniture and fabric. Create enough yardage to construct curtains, cushions, or even a shower curtain. Imagine a painted plaid design on wooden chair seats or a freestanding wooden cabinet. It is always a good idea to test your plaid design on paper or a scrap piece of fabric.

MATERIALS NEEDED
- foam minirollers
- small paint tray
- acrylic or latex paint (for furniture)
- textile paint (for fabrics)
- utility knife
- drop cloth

DIRECTIONS

1. If painting plaid on fabric, prepare the fabric as directed by the manufacturer of the paints you are using. If painting plaid on furniture, sand the wood until smooth and prime it with white primer. If necessary, sand the surface again to be sure it is smooth.

2. Notch the rollers with a utility knife to create sections. These sections can be symmetrical or asymmetrical (fig. 1).

Figure 1

3. Assign one color of paint to each roller. Apply the brightest or darkest color first. You don't have to wait between colors because the wet paints may blend together to create a completely new color. If you want to keep with a planned color scheme and don't want any color surprises, allow each color application to dry before applying another layer.

4. Roll lines vertically and horizontally across surface to achieve different plaid effects (fig. 2).

5. Follow the manufacturer's suggestions for permanently setting fabric paints. For wood pieces, apply several coats of polyurethane; allow it to dry between applications and sand lightly before additional coats are applied.

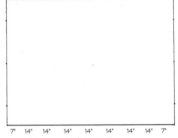

Figure 2

How To Paint Diamonds on Walls

MATERIALS NEEDED
- latex paint in two colors
- metal measuring tape
- straight edge
- painter's masking tape, 3/4 inches wide
- pencil
- chalk line
- calculator
- stepladder

Figure 1

DIRECTIONS

1. Paint the entire wall with the color of your choice.

2. To determine the width of each diamond, choose an odd number of diamonds (1, 3, 5,) to fit across the wall. Then divide the odd number into the width of the wall. Repeat this process for the length of the diamond.

3. Divide the width of the diamond in half. Begin at the ceiling along one edge or in a corner and make a tick mark at this measurement. Continue marking the full width of each diamond. You will end with the half diamond measurement when you get to the opposite corner (fig. 1). Repeat this process using the length of the diamonds along both sides of the wall.

Figure 2

4. Use a chalk line to connect diagonal guidelines. Continue until the entire wall is divided into diamonds (fig. 2).

5. Apply tape along the outside of every diamond to be painted; cover the chalk lines with tape (fig. 3).

6. Paint the diamonds and allow them to dry. Remove tape.

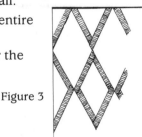

Figure 3

How To Paint Stripes on Walls

It's not a difficult process to paint stripes on walls if you follow these suggestions.

MATERIALS NEEDED
- satin latex paint in two colors of your choice
- small paint rollers or wide foam brushes

- level
- tape measure
- painter's tape (3 inches wide)
- string, plumb line, plumb bob, and chalk

DIRECTIONS

1. Fix any cracks or holes with a spackling compound and sand those surfaces smooth. Paint the entire wall in the lighter of the two stripe colors. Let dry completely.

2. Make a tick mark at the center of the wall's width; then in even increments out from the center mark stripes in the desired width—usually every 5 to 12 inches. Measure accurately. Use a level to make sure the lines are true.

3. Using the plumb line, mark vertical stripes on the wall.

4. Mask off every other line with 3-inch-wide low-tack painter's tape. Rub a thumbnail along each edge of the tape to prevent paint from leaking under the tape.

5. Using a foam brush or miniroller, fill in between the stripes with the darker paint. Allow the paint to dry before removing the tape. Do not leave tape on the wall overnight or it will begin to pull up the undercoat of paint.

Design Option 1: Ragging Off

"Color wash" the stripe with a mixture of clear latex glaze and the second paint color (or substitute this combination with a pretinted glaze in the color of your choice). If making your own glaze, the proportions of paint to glaze can differ—it depends on the look you want. In general, a mixture that is more than half glaze is more translucent, and one that is less than half glaze is more opaque. Apply the mixture with a sponge or nylon brush; work in small sections. Pat the painted area with a damp cotton rag gathered into a ball until you get the desired texture. Let paint dry and remove the tape.

Design Option 2: Combing

Apply a paint/glaze mixture as the second stripe and, while the glaze is still wet, drag a combing tool down each glazed stripe.

How To Paint Tri-Color Stripes

If you are more adventurous, try this tri-color technique on your walls.

MATERIALS NEEDED
- paint roller
- latex paint in three colors (see below)
- paint tray
- level
- cardboard
- pencil

DIRECTIONS

1. Select three colors you want to use. This technique works best if these three colors are from the same paint chip strip. Paint the entire wall the lightest of the three colors. Allow to dry.

2. Measure the paint roller you are using. Make a painting plan by marking the width of the roller across the wall you are painting. Make very light vertical lines at each of these marks. This painting technique will not produce rigid stripes, so these plumb lines are only a guideline to keep your stripes vertical.

3. Cut two pieces of cardboard that follow the contour of the length of the paint tray. These will act as paint dividers.

4. Divide the tray into three compartments by taping the cardboard dividers in place at each end. Fill the two outside compartments with two different colors. Fill the center section with the lightest color.

5. Quickly remove the dividers; be careful not to drip the paint from the cardboard back into the tray.

6. Load your roller as you would for any painting project. Roll the three colors onto the wall in long, single-direction strokes. Do not use a back-and-forth motion or you will lose the stripes. To reload the roller, put it in the tray with the colors lined up so they don't become blended.

7. Add more paint as needed to the tray by replacing the dividers and filling the compartments as described in step 4.

How To Paint a Geometric Wall Quilt

If you love the look of a quilt on the wall but are not handy with a needle and thread, you can paint a quilt on the wall—no sewing involved. The easiest quilt design to paint uses stripes or squares or triangles or any combination of the three. Below are directions for a center diamond quilt, but you can certainly paint any quilt design you want. Wonderful resources for solid-color geometric quilt designs are books on Amish quilts. Special quilt shops or your library should have these resources.

MATERIALS NEEDED
(finished size:
46 inches square)

- paintbrushes, 1 1/2 inches wide
- painter's masking tape
- latex or acrylic paints in colors of your choice
- latex or acrylic paint, flat black (small amount)
- optional: quilt design book
- pencil
- level

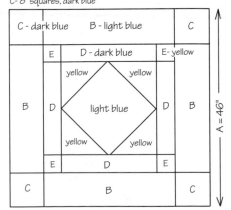

A- square 46"
B- 8" borders, light blue
C- 8" squares, dark blue
D- 4" inside borders, dark blue
E- 4" squares, yellow

DIRECTIONS

1. With a light pencil and a level, draw a 46-inch square on your wall. This square is the perimeter of your wall quilt.

2. Then draw an 8-inch outer border inside the perimeter of the quilt. Extend the line into the corners to create 8-inch corner squares.

3. Draw another border inside the first border, 4 inches wide, again with corner squares.

4. Inside the center square, draw a square on point—that is, a diamond—by marking the halfway point of each side and connecting the marks.

5. Assign the colors to each section of your quilt. Use the finished diagram in this book and colored markers to work out the colors.

6. Carefully mask off the outside edges of the first color to be painted with painter's tape. With your fingernail, press the edges of the tape tightly to the wall to prevent paint from seeping into adjoining areas.
Tip: Leave the other edge of the tape loose for easy removal.

7. Paint one color at a time. Apply the first color of paint. Remove the tape and allow the paint to dry completely.

8. Repeat the process with the additional colors.

9. With flat black paint, paint a $3/8$-inch-wide border around the outside edge of the quilt.

How To Create Crosshatching

This technique is especially effective when soft, warm colors are used.

MATERIALS NEEDED
- two 4-inch paintbrushes
- paper towels
- satin or gloss latex paint for the basecoat
- one or two additional shades of paint colors from the same color card

DIRECTIONS

1. Paint the entire wall the base color. Allow it to dry overnight.

2. Mix together paint and water for the first crosshatching color. Experiment to find the proportions you like best. However, a good starting point is one part paint to two parts water. For a more translucent look, add more water.

3. Apply this coat in sweeping diagonally crisscrossed strokes about 6 inches in length; use an almost-dry paintbrush. Dip the tip of the brush into the mixture and then dab off the excess onto a paper towel. Cover the entire wall with crisscrosses, leaving obvious spaces so the basecoat shows (about 40 percent).

4. Repeat the process with the third color. Apply this color with the same dry-brush technique used for the previous crosshatches. This coat should cover your basecoat and portions of the previous color's brush strokes.

How To Apply a Combed Finish

MATERIALS NEEDED
- wide paint roller
- clear latex glaze
- satin or gloss latex paint for the basecoat
- satin or gloss latex paint for the top coat
- window squeegee or combing tool from paint or craft store

DIRECTIONS

Note: This technique works just as well on furniture.

1. Paint the entire wall the base color. Allow it to dry overnight.

2. Fashion a comb from the squeegee by cutting teeth into the rubber portion of the squeegee, or use a tool specially made for this technique.

3. Mix glaze and top coat color together; follow manufacturer's instructions for suggested proportions.

4. The following steps require two people to complete the process successfully. The first person rolls on the top coat color from ceiling to floor. Beginning at the ceiling, the second person immediately combs through the paint in one long stroke. If you want to create a checkerboard pattern, comb crosswise over this section at planned intervals.

5. Repeat this process across the entire width of the wall. Comb the whole wall without stopping.

6. For best results, apply even pressure on the comb and work quickly. Wipe the comb frequently to prevent paint build-up.

How To Paint Faux Terra Cotta Tile

Use this technique on concrete floors and entryways.

MATERIALS NEEDED
- utility knife
- craft glue
- rubber gloves
- pencil
- ruler
- cardboard squares, each 12 inches
- foam squares ($1/2$ inch thick), each 12 inches
- 2 large squares of cardboard (at least 20 inches)
- latex paint: three colors of terra cotta (light, medium, and dark)
- latex floor and patio paint, medium gray
- clear latex satin-finish urethane

DIRECTIONS

1. Wash the floor surface.

2. Apply a basecoat to the floor by painting the surface with a gray-colored floor-and-patio paint.

3. Make a tile "stamp" by gluing $1/2$-inch foam to a 12-inch square of cardboard. Allow the floor and stamp to dry overnight. Note: If placing the tile in a diagonal pattern, prepare separate triangular corner applicators.

4. Determine the pattern of tile placement and mark guidelines on the floor.

5. On the large piece of cardboard, mix the three terra cotta–colored paints together to achieve subtle blending.

6. Press the stamp into swirled paint, and lightly blot any excess onto a piece of

scrap cardboard. Press the first square onto the floor; make sure all areas of the stamp are pressed evenly. Lift the stamp, give it a 1/4 turn, and press a second "tile" onto the floor surface. Leave a 1/2-inch space between the tiles to simulate a grout line. Repeat until the entire surface is covered.

7. Allow the floor to dry completely before applying two or three coats of clear satin-finish urethane.

How To Make a Chalkboard

Use a special chalkboard spray found in home centers and large craft departments to create a one-of-a-kind chalkboard for your children.

MATERIALS NEEDED
- chalkboard spray paint
- 3-inch-wide fluted molding
- 3/4-inch-wide cove molding
- 2-inch-wide crown molding
- painter's masking tape
- wood glue
- pencil
- level
- yardstick
- drop cloth
- assorted nails
- hammer

DIRECTIONS

1. Along one wall, mark a 12-to-14-inch-wide band at a comfortable height for your child. This is the size of the chalkboard.

2. Tape off the band with painter's tape.

3. Apply chalkboard paint following the manufacturer's instructions for proper ventilation, application guidelines, and recommended drying time.

4. For the chalk ledge, cut the molding into lengths equal to the length of the painted chalkboard. Paint the molding as desired.

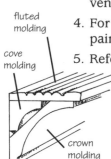

fluted molding

cove molding

crown molding

5. Refer to the diagram to see ledge assembly. First, nail the cove molding to the wall along the bottom edge of the chalkboard. Nail the fluted molding to the top edge of the cove molding. Predrill pilot holes into the crown molding. Run a bead of wood glue along the top edge of the crown molding and secure it in place under the fluted molding and against the wall. Nail through the crown and cove molding into the wall. Fill the nail holes and touch up with paint.

How To Construct a Shaker-Style Peg Shelf

MATERIALS NEEDED
- two 1-by-4-inch pine boards, cut to the desired shelf length (one for the shelf and one for the peg board)
- 2-inch-long miniature Shaker pegs (placed approximately 6 inches apart)
- wood glue
- drill
- finishing nails
- hammer
- measuring tape
- sandpaper
- tack cloth
- paint or stain

DIRECTIONS

1. Sand the edges of the 1-by-4-inch boards. Remove dust particles with the tack cloth.

2. Glue and nail the shelf to the peg board at a 90 degree angle. The top flat edge of the shelf should be flush with the top of the peg board.

3. Drill holes for the pegs about 6 inches apart and 1 1/2 inches from the bottom edge of the peg board. (Test for the proper drill bit size on a scrap piece of wood. The pegs should fit snugly.) After peg holes are drilled, dab wood glue to end of each peg and insert it into its hole. Allow the shelf to dry.

4. Paint, stain, or antique as desired.

How To **Make a Baseball Hat Valance**

MATERIALS NEEDED
- drill and drill bit
- wood glue
- length of 1-by-6-inch wood
- wooden dowel, 3/4-inch diameter

DIRECTIONS

1. Drill 3/4-inch holes (about 7 inches apart) into a piece of 1-by-6-inch wood equal to the width of the window plus 3 inches.

2. Cut the wooden dowel into 4-inch lengths. Dab wood glue to the end of each peg and insert it into its hole. Allow the glue to dry.

3. Paint or finish the valance as desired.

4. Center and attach it over the top of the window frame. Hang your hats from the dowels.

How To **Make a Shutter Screen with Shelving**

Shutters of all sizes can be made into room dividers. The addition of shelves makes the screen an interesting display area.

MATERIALS NEEDED
- door or window shutters
- bifold hinges
- shelf supports
- sandpaper
- wood glue
- finishing nails
- mounting hooks, two per shelf
- pine shelving to fit the width of shutters
- hammer
- wood putty
- primer
- spray-paint
- screwdriver

DIRECTIONS

1. Cut shelves to equal lengths. Sand the ends smooth.

2. To attach a shelf to supports, apply wood glue to the top edges of two brackets. Then glue the brackets to the underside of the shelf about 1/2 inch from each short end. Allow the glue to dry.

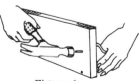

Figure 1

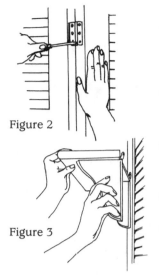

Figure 2

Figure 3

3. For extra security, hammer finishing nails through the top of the shelf into the supports (fig. 1). To camouflage the nail hole, fill it with wood putty. Allow the putty to dry. Then sand it smooth.

4. Paint the shutters, shelves, and shelf supports in the color of your choice before assembly. Allow the paint to dry completely before assembling.

5. Attach hinges to the side edges of the shutters (fig. 2). Place the hinges about 4 inches from each end and in the center of each shutter. Install the hinges using package instructions.

6. Position the shelves on the shutters where desired and mark the positions.

7. Attach mounting hooks to the back of each shelf and position two nails in corresponding positions on each shutter. Attach the shelves by sliding the hooks over the nails (fig. 3).

How To Dye Furniture

Traditional household dye can be used to create a rich and colorful finish on any unfinished wood, wicker, or straw items.

MATERIALS NEEDED
- unfinished wood piece
- container for making dye
- sponge paintbrushes
- plastic drop cloth
- cotton rags (old T-shirts work well)
- household dye (Rit or Dylon are two popular brand names)
- tack cloth
- clear polyurethane
- rubber gloves
- sandpaper

DIRECTIONS

1. Make sure any finishes (paint, varnish, or wax) are removed from the object being dyed. Sand wood pieces until smooth and wipe with tack cloth.

2. Mix dye following the manufacturer's instructions.

3. Test the dye solution on an unobtrusive area to be sure the color is what you planned; the color may be darker than desired until the item is completely dry.

4. Apply dye to the surface in the direction of the grain; use a sponge brush for large surfaces. Keep a clean cloth nearby to clean up any drips. If the dye accidentally flows into the wrong area, wipe it off immediately and use sandpaper to remove the dye. After dye is applied, wipe away any excess.

5. When the piece is completely dry, seal it with two coats of polyurethane. Sand the item lightly between coats and wipe it clean with a lint-free cloth.

Design Option 1: Aging

If you want uneven color coverage to make your project look more "aged," wait until the dye is semidry and then wipe some of the dye away. After the project is completely dry, you can continue to age it by lightly sanding the surface; vary the pressure to create an uneven look.

Design Option 2: Stenciling

After the project is completely dry, you can also stencil with dye. Make sure the stencil is firmly adhered to the surface.

How To Make a Lace-Stenciled Table

The illusion of a lace tablecloth can be created with spray-paints and lace doilies. This technique also works well on bureaus, headboards, nightstands, kitchen cabinets, or bookcases.

MATERIALS NEEDED
- kitchen table
- repositionable spray adhesive
- two coordinating colors in spray-paint
- paper doilies
- primer
- sandpaper

DIRECTIONS

1. When selecting paper doilies, consider overall shape, size, and intricacy. Doilies are available in many shapes: circles, squares, hearts, and rectangles.

2. Prime the surface of a wood table after sanding it smooth. After the prime coat has dried, you may need to sand lightly again to ensure a smooth surface.

3. Apply paint to the wood surface. The color of the paint will be the color of the doily imprint. For example, if the first coat is painted light blue, and the second coat is lemon yellow, the doilies will be blue. Allow the first coat to dry.

4. Plan the design of the "tablecloth" by arranging doilies as desired. When you are pleased with the arrangement, spray the smooth side of the doily with repositionable spray adhesive. Press the doilies in place; make sure all edges adhere to the table surface so the paint won't run under them.

5. Spray the entire surface with the second color of paint. Allow it to dry. Remove the doilies.

6. If necessary, use a small brush to touch up any area where a doily may have slipped.

How To Apply Wallpaper Borders to Furniture

Adding wallpaper border accents to an old piece of furniture gives it a whole new life.

MATERIALS NEEDED
- wooden furniture (with straight edges)
- wallpaper border (choose a width that will complement the dimensions of your table)
- optional: wallpaper paste if the border is not prepasted
- craft knife
- straight edge

- sandpaper
- polyurethane
- soft cotton cloth
- latex paint
- steel wool

DIRECTIONS

1. Repair any nicks or dents on the furniture surface with wood putty. Be sure to match the existing color of the wood.

2. Sand the entire surface smooth and paint or stain as desired. A combination of both of these techniques is very attractive. For example, paint the legs of a table and stain the tabletop. Or if you prefer, paint the entire surface.

3. Select a wallpaper border that is in proportion with the furniture piece you are covering.

4. If applying a wallpaper border to the perimeter of a table surface, measure in and mark a distance equal to the width of the border from the outside edge.

5. Measure and cut the border to fit each side of the table; allow extra on both ends of each strip for mitering (the amount depends on the width of the border you are using). Miter the corners by placing the ends across each other at a 90 degree angle. Use a utility knife and a straight edge to cut through both strips at a 45 degree angle. Double check the fit of the border around the perimeter.

6. Apply the wallpaper border to the table; follow the marked line.

7. Wipe away all excess glue or paste with a warm, wet sponge. Allow the paper to dry thoroughly (at least 24 hours). Apply three coats of polyurethane to the surface; allow it to dry completely between each application. Then sand and wipe each layer clean with steel wool and a soft cloth.

Design Option: Applying wallpaper or borders to drawer fronts.

Remove knobs and paint the entire surface in a color to match the selected wallpaper or border. For a better bond, sand the drawer fronts lightly before applying wallpaper or border. Apply wallpaper or border that has been trimmed to size. Replace knobs. Clean the project and apply polyurethane as explained above.

How To Finger-Paint on Furniture

Reminiscent of childhood years, try finger-painting designs on your furniture surface. This is a mistake-proof project! If you think you have made a mistake, the "open time" of the glaze before it dries (10 to 15 minutes) allows you to start again.

MATERIALS NEEDED
- furniture
- clear latex glaze
- latex paint in two colors of your choice
- foam brush
- clear varnish

DIRECTIONS

1. Items to be painted need to be clean and dry. Apply basecoat to the entire surface with the lighter of the two selected colors and an ordinary paintbrush. Allow the paint to dry completely.

2. Apply a color wash that is made from a mixture of clear latex glaze and the second paint color. Apply the mixture with a foam brush; work in small sections.

3. Finger-paint while the glaze is still wet. If you don't like what you have done, simply recoat the area with glaze (while it is still wet) and begin your painted masterpiece again.

4. Once the glaze is dry, apply a coat of clear varnish over it to protect your work.

How To Make a Napkin Chair Cover

These chair covers are so easy to make, consider making several for seasonal and holiday changes.

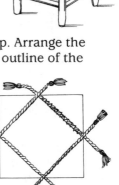

MATERIALS NEEDED
(for each chair)

- two 20-inch square cloth napkins
- high-loft batting square (to fit top of chair)
- four 27-inch tasseled tiebacks
- thread to match tiebacks
- erasable fabric marker

DIRECTIONS

1. Place one napkin diagonally on top of the chair seat, right side up. Arrange the corners of the napkin to hang off the edges of the seat. Mark the outline of the chair seat onto the napkin with a fabric marker.

2. Cut a piece of batting to fit the outlined shape of the chair. Place the batting against the wrong side of the marked napkin within the marked outline.

3. Pin napkins wrong sides together with the batting sandwiched in between. Stitch through all layers directly on the marked line.

4. Center tasseled tiebacks along each stitching line; tassels should be an even distance from the corners. Zigzag stitch over the cording tieback, keeping the tassels free (see figure).

5. Place the cushion on the chair and tie it at each corner with the tasseled ends.

How To Replace Outdoor Chair Covers

Don't throw away folding chairs with torn webbing. Paint the chair frame a refreshing new color and attach a piece of coordinated fabric to replace the torn webbing.

MATERIALS NEEDED
- sewing machine
- plastic rope, 1/4-inch
- grommets, 3/8-inch
- rust-proof primer
- grommet pliers or insertion kit
- spray-paint in color of your choice
- heavyweight, tightly woven fabric (canvas, denim, tapestry)
- lawn chair
- scissors
- sandpaper

DIRECTIONS

1. Remove existing webbing; save the screws for the new cover.

2. Clean the chair, removing rust, dirt, and grime. Prime the frame with rust-resistant primer. Paint the chair in the color of your choice.

3. Measure the chair to determine the amount of fabric you need. To determine the width of the chair seat, measure the width of the chair and add 4 inches. To determine the length of the chair cover, measure from the top rail, down the chair back to the front rail and add 6 inches (fig. 1). Cut two rectangles to these dimensions.

Figure 1

4. To determine the number of grommets, measure from the top rail to the seat and from the seat to the front rail. Plan for a grommet to be inserted about every 2 inches. Double the number of grommets for both sides.

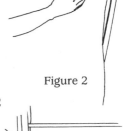

Figure 2

5. On the long edges of each rectangle, fold under and press 2 inches toward the wrong side of the fabric. Then place the rectangles wrong sides together with folded edges matching. Stitch along both long sides 1 3/4 inches from the folded edge. Then stitch another row of stitching along the edge.

6. Arrange the rectangle to go over the front of the top bar. Fold under the raw edges along the back of the bar. Attach the chair cover to the chair with the saved screws (fig. 2).

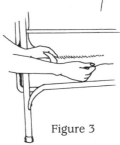

Figure 3

7. The fabric cover should now go under the center rail and over the front rail. Pull it taut. Attach the chair cover to the front rail with the rest of the saved screws (fig. 3).

8. Make marks for grommet placement along both long edges about 2 inches apart. Insert the grommets; follow the manufacturer's instructions.

9. Thread rope through the top grommets and around the side bars on each side; work back to front. Pull the rope taut to keep the chair cover from sagging. Tie a knot underneath the front of the chair. Trim the ends of the rope (fig. 4).

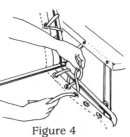

Figure 4

How To Decoupage under Glass

Use this technique to create a unique glass tabletop.

MATERIALS NEEDED
- sheet of glass (available in home centers and glass and mirror shops)
- photographs, sheet music, old letters, postcards, and so on
- PVA adhesive (available at art supply stores)
- scissors
- grease pencil
- craft knife
- white spray-paint
- polyurethane
- paintbrush

DIRECTIONS

1. Take your paper images to a copy center and make photocopies in color or black and white. Enlarge and reduce the images to vary the sizes. Note: Copy centers may be reluctant to copy images from books because of the copyright. However, if you use old books (at least 75 years old), chances are the copyright has expired and the pictures are in the public domain.

2. Arrange the copied images face up on a large work surface. Place the glass over the arrangement, right side up. With a grease pencil, outline each image for future reference.

3. Turn glass wrong side up on large surface. Glue the photocopies to this side of the glass with PVA adhesive. Apply the glue to the right side of the copied images. Press the images in place; make sure the edges adhere to glass surface securely. Allow them to dry thoroughly.

4. Once dry, turn the glass over and trim any protruding images flush with the edge of the glass.

5. Turn the glass wrong side up. Apply painter's masking tape around the edges of the glass. Spray paint the back of the glass with white spray paint. When it is dry, apply a coat of polyurethane. Remove the masking tape. Allow the top of the tabletop to dry for several days before using it.

How To Cover Surfaces with Mosaic Tiles

Create a mosaic table by using tiny pieces of broken tile, dishes, or colored glass. Flea markets and secondhand stores are excellent resources for inexpensive dishware. Plates or platters are the best pieces to use as they will produce the most flat pieces when broken.

MATERIALS NEEDED
- tile, dishes, or colored glass
- large plastic resealable bag
- ceramic tile adhesive
- narrow wood molding
- grout in a color of your choice
- hammer
- towel
- trowel
- damp sponge
- grout seal

DIRECTIONS

1. Optional: Form a "frame" around the perimeter of the tabletop by attaching narrow wood molding along the outside edges. Use glue and small finishing nails.

2. Paint the furniture piece in a color of your choice.

3. Break tiles, dishes, or glass into small pieces. *Protect your eyes—wear goggles!* Put a tile or dish in a plastic zip-locked bag placed inside a towel and break it into smaller pieces with a hammer.

4. Working in small sections, spread a layer of ceramic tile adhesive over a portion of the table surface. Press pieces of broken tile into the adhesive. Add adhesive and tile until entire surface is covered. Note: If you are using dish fragments, apply a thicker adhesive coat because the pieces aren't flat. Allow the table to dry at least 24 hours before proceeding. Allow extra drying time if you applied thicker adhesive.

5. Mix the grout according to the manufacturer's directions. The grout should be the consistency of peanut butter. Spread the grout over the tiles; use a trowel. Go over the area two or three times to force the grout into the spaces between tiles. All joints should be full of grout and level with the tiles. Remove as much excess grout as possible by dragging the edge of a trowel across the tiles. Allow the grout to dry.

6. Wipe off excess grout with a *damp* sponge. Do not allow the grout to get too wet. After a few hours, clean the tiles again with a damp sponge.

7. Apply grout seal; follow manufacturer's instructions.

How To Cover a Window Box with Tile

MATERIALS NEEDED
- wooden window box
- tile adhesive
- enough tiles to cover the surface of the window box
- notched trowel
- grout

DIRECTIONS

1. Measure the box to determine the number of decorative tiles you'll need.

2. Apply a layer of adhesive with the smooth edge of the notched trowel. Then draw the notched edge over the adhesive to create grooves.

3. Press the tiles in place; twist them into position so they grip the adhesive. Place the tiles apart slightly if necessary to adjust them to fit the box.

4. Allow the adhesive to dry before applying grout.

5. Spread grout over the tiles; fill in the spaces.

6. Wipe off excess grout with a damp sponge. Allow the grout to dry and then remove the haze with a soft cloth.

How To Create a Verdigris Urn

Verdigris is a faux finish that is applied to a surface to create the look of aged and discolored copper. Note: This same technique can be used on a decorative wall plaque or statue.

MATERIALS NEEDED
- flat black latex paint
- aqua latex paint
- clear spray sealer
- ceramic urn, statue, or wall plaque (select a piece that has lots of cracks and crevices for best results)
- latex glazing liquid
- rags

DIRECTIONS

1. Apply flat black latex paint to the entire surface. Allow it to dry completely.

2. Prepare the top coat by mixing four parts aqua latex paint with one part glazing liquid.

3. Apply the top coat in a baseball-card sized area. Immediately after applying the top coat, crumple a rag and gently blot and dab the paint with it. Begin at the outside edges and soften the lines, then work to the middle. Remove as much paint as desired until you get the look you want. Continue until the entire surface is covered.

4. When it's dry, seal the piece with three coats of clear spray sealer; allow it to dry between coats.

How To Design Your Own Flowerpots

MATERIALS NEEDED
- plain clay flowerpots and saucers
- assorted acrylic paints (for a 4-ounce flowerpot, you'll need one 1-ounce jar for the basecoat and three 1-ounce jars of different colors for designs)
- clear acrylic sealer (spray or liquid)
- one or more of the following: small sponge paintbrush, small makeup sponge, artist's brush, cotton swabs, felt-tip markers

DIRECTIONS

1. Begin with a clean pot. If you are using old pots, scrub off the dirt. If you are using a new pot, wipe it with a damp cloth to remove any dust. Allow the pot to dry before beginning.

2. Apply a thin layer of sealer to the pot and saucer and allow it to dry.

3. Paint the entire pot and saucer with basecoat. Let them dry for one hour.

4. Decorate the pot as desired. Apply straight or curvy lines with foam or artist's brushes; sponge on geometric shapes using makeup sponges dipped in paint; randomly place polka dots using the cotton swabs; add names or personal messages with felt-tip markers.

Glossary

A

Accent color – A contrasting color used to enliven a room.

Accordion pleat – A method of fan folding fabric or paper.

Angle bracket – An L-shaped piece of metal on which shelving is supported on a wall.

Antique (verb) – A process used to simulate wear and tear on surfaces.

Art Deco – A historic design period (1909 to 1939).

B

Backsaw – A saw with metal ribs along its back.

Back splash – A protective covering for the area just above the kitchen sink.

Battenburg lace – A type of lace characterized by tape stitched in a design to linen.

Batting – A fluffy substance used for padding; available prepackaged or by the yard.

Blinds – A type of window treatment, usually with horizontal slats, such as a miniblind.

Bullion fringe – Edging, made of long twisted cords and used on upholstery, slipcovers, pillow covers, etc.

C

Café rings – Decorative rings that slide onto rods to hold café curtains in place.

Camelback – A style of sofa that mimics the humped shape of a camel's back.

Carpenter's square – An L-shaped measuring device that enables one to measure length and width simultaneously.

C-clamp – A device in the shape of a C designed to press two or more parts together.

Ceiling panels – Individual panels used primarily for drop ceilings.

Chair rail – Decorative molding attached to wall at chair height; originally used to protect walls from being scratched by the backs of chairs, it is now used mainly for decorative purposes.

Colorfast – The ability of fabric to resist fading.

Color washing – A decorative painting technique in which a very thin, almost transparent layer of glaze is applied to a surface.

Glossary

Combing – A decorative painting technique where combs are dragged through glaze to create texture.

Cordovan – The color of soft leather.

Cornice – A window treatment that covers the top portion of a window; usually made from wood and covered with fabric.

Cove molding – A type of concave molding.

Crosshatching – The application of several coats of a translucent glaze applied in a crisscrossed pattern over a basecoat.

Crown molding – A wide molding that projects into the room; used primarily around ceilings.

Cut length – The measurement of the fabric that equals the vertical length plus any allowances for hems or seams.

Cut width – The measurement of the fabric from side edge to side edge after widths of fabric are stitched together but before any construction has begun.

D

Decal – A picture or design made to be temporarily transferred to a hard surface.

Decoupage – A technique using cutouts of paper or fabric applied to various surfaces and coated with varnish for permanence.

Dovetail joint – An interlocking joint between two pieces of wood.

Drop-leaf table – A table with hinged leaves that can be folded down.

Duvet – A comforter.

E

Eggshell – Oil or water-based paint with a low-sheen finish; also known as satin or low-luster.

Embossed – Having a raised ornamental surface.

Epoxy glue – A glue made from epoxy, a strong bonding agent.

Eyelet – A circular metal ring pressed through fabric through which a cord is pulled.

F

Faux – A term used to describe a finish that simulates something that it's not; usually achieved with decorative paint techniques.

Ferrule – A metal ring around a wooden paintbrush used for additional strength.

Fiberfill – Loose, soft filling used to stuff pillows, dolls, stuffed animals.

Finial – An ornamental accent used at the end of curtain rods or the top of a bedpost.

Finishing nails – Nails with small, unobtrusive heads.

Florist foam – A firm spongy product, also known as oasis, used when arranging flowers.

Fuse – Adhering two layers together with a bonding agent and heat (usually from an iron).

Fusible web – A bonding agent that holds two layers of fabric together when heat is applied.

G

Gesso – A paste-like substance that is applied to surfaces to make them suitable for painting.

Glazing – A decorative paint technique in which a film of color is applied to a surface to create a semitransparent effect.

Gloss (paint) – A type of paint that dries to a high sheen.

Glue gun – An electric device used for assembly of crafts. Sticks of special glue are inserted into an opening and then heated to melt the glue.

Grease pencil – A marking device that is used on smooth surfaces such as glass.

Grit (of sandpaper; i.e., 60-grit) – An indication of the degree of fineness. The higher the number, the finer the paper.

Grommets – Large eyelets or metal rings pressed through fabric.

Grosgrain (ribbon) – Woven ribbon that has a cross-rib design.

Grout – A thin mortar used to fill spaces between tile pieces.

H

Homosote – A building material that has a porous surface.

Hook-and-loop tape – A type of fastener that has thread like "hooks" on one side and thread like "loops" on the other; the two sides adhere to each other when pressed together.

Hue – The name of a color such as blue, green, or yellow.

I

Intensity (of color) – The amount of saturation of a color. For example, red has a higher intensity than pink.

J

Jabot – Folded fabric that hangs vertically.

L

Lacquer – A hard varnish that is applied in several layers then polished for a high sheen.

Leading – In stained glass, the dividing substance between pieces of colored glass.

Level – A device used to determine if a surface is in the horizontal plane.

Linseed oil – A yellowish oil used on furniture.

Liquid seam sealant – A liquid that, when applied to the cut edge of fabric, will eliminate fraying.

Louvers – Slats of wood fixed or movable in a framed opening such as a door or window.

Low-luster (paint) – Oil or water-based paint with a low-sheen finish; also known as eggshell or satin paint.

Low-tack painter's tape – Masking tape with a special adhesive that won't remove paint when the tape is removed.

M

Mandarin braid – A wide dimensional braid that is used to embellish place mats, pillows, and other home decor accessories.

Marbling – A decorative painting technique used to create the look of real marble.

Marquetry – Inlaid decorative detail found on furniture or decorative wooden accessories.

Mat/mat board – A colored cardboard frame that surrounds a picture or photograph in a frame.

Mineral spirits – A liquid found in hardware stores; used to clean paintbrushes.

Miter – The angle formed by joining two pieces of wood or fabric to make a 90 degree angle.

Miter box – A stabilizing device used when cutting pieces of wood into precise angles; usually with slotted sides to guide a handsaw.

Glossary

Moiré – Fabric, usually silk, that has a wavy pattern that gives a rippled appearance.

Molding – Strips of wood or other materials applied to walls, doors, ceilings, and furniture for decorative effect.

Molly bolt – A wall anchor with elbows that flare out when it is screwed in; used on hollow walls where wood-framing studs are absent.

Monochromatic – A color scheme that contains shades of one color only.

Motif – A single design or decorative pattern within a larger design.

N

Nail set – A tool used to recess the head of a nail (usually a "finish" nail) below the surface of the wood.

O

Opaque projector – A piece of equipment that projects images in a large scale on a wall.

P

Patina – A change of surface appearance, usually caused by age or wear, that can be achieved artificially through a decorative painting technique.

Peg molding – Molding in which wooden pegs have been inserted; often for hanging items.

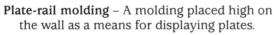

Plate-rail molding – A molding placed high on the wall as a means for displaying plates.

Plumb bob – A heavy object tied to a cord to create a plumb line.

Plumb line – A straight vertical line from the ceiling to the floor. The device used to determine such a line; usually a string with a plumb bob.

Pole rods – Decorative rods for window treatments that have no exterior working mechanisms.

Polyurethane – A synthetic resin used in varnish; used for protection from moisture.

Preshrunk – A term for fabric that has been subjected to a shrinking process during manufacturing.

Press cloth – Fabric that is placed between an iron and decorating fabric for protection against scorching and iron shine.

Primary colors – The three colors that make all other colors (red, yellow, and blue).

R

Ragging on/ragging off – Decorative painting techniques. In ragging on, a rag is dipped into a glaze or paint and used to apply a textured pattern. In ragging off, a rag is used to remove wet paint.

Rag roll – A decorative painting technique that uses a rag that has been twisted into a sausage shape and rolled over a wet surface for texture.

Riser – The vertical portion on a step.

Roman shade – A flat fabric window treatment that folds up accordion-style from the bottom.

Rottenstone – Decomposed limestone used for polishing.

Rung – A rounded piece of wood that is placed between the legs of a chair for stability; also, a crosspiece of a ladder.

S

Satin (paint) – Oil or water-based paint with a low-sheen finish; also known as eggshell or low-luster.

Sconce – A decorative wall-mounted bracket designed to support a drapery rod, shelf, or swagged fabric.

Seam allowance – The area that extends from the stitching line to the cut outer edge of a sewn item.

Seam roller – A tool used to adhere wallpaper edges to the wall.

Secondary colors – Colors made by combining two primary colors. There are three secondary colors: green (made from blue and yellow), orange (made from red and yellow), and purple (made from red and blue).

Self-adhesive – Wallpaper or vinyl with an adhesive, usually activated with water, that was applied during the manufacturing process.

Selvage – The finished edges of fabric that run down both sides.

Semi-gloss – A relatively low-luster paint that is midway between gloss and flat.

Shade (color) – The degree of darkness of a color.

Shade (window) – A vinyl or cloth window treatment that covers the glass area of a window; commonly rolls to the top on a spring-type roller mechanism.

Sheers – Transparent fabrics.

Shellac – A liquid substance that is used as a wood finish.

Shirred – Gathered.

Sisal (rug) – A rug made from a strong fiber that has been made into a cord.

Slipcovers – Removable fabric covers for furniture pieces.

Smooshing – A decorative painting and texturing technique in which a wet paint or glaze is removed with a plastic sheet that has been applied to the area and then removed.

Spackle – A brand of surfacing compound. A powdered mixture that is mixed with water to create a paste and used as a filler for cracks.

Spattering – A decorative painting technique that is created by tapping or flicking paint from a toothbrush onto a plain surface.

Sponging – A decorative painting technique involving the application of one or more layers of paint with a sponge.

Spring-tension rod – A curtain or shower curtain rod that is mounted between two walls without brackets; the rod is contracted to fit inside an area and, when released, will put pressure against the walls and stay secure.

Squeegee – A blade of rubber used for spreading or removing paint or other liquids from a flat surface.

Stenciling – Creating patterns by masking off areas of a surface and then applying color to the exposed areas.

Stippling – A painting technique that is used for stenciling or to soften and blend colors.

Surfacing compound – See Spackle.

Swag – A draped fabric window treatment.

Swag rings – Specially designed window treatment hardware used to hold fabric so it can drape gracefully over an area.

T

Table topper – Additional layer of fabric primarily used for decorative purposes that is placed over coordinating table covering.

Glossary

Tabs – Extensions of fabric that are formed into loops or ties used to hold a curtain rod.

Tack cloth – A sticky cloth available in hardware and paint stores; used to remove any dust particles that result from sanding.

Tatting – Delicate handmade lace.

Tempera – A nontoxic water-based craft paint traditionally used for posters.

Tertiary colors – Combinations of primary and secondary colors. There are six tertiary colors: red-orange, yellow-orange, blue-green, yellow-green, red-violet, and blue-violet.

Tieback – A decorative fastener made from fabric or other materials that is attached to the side of the window to hold back curtains or draperies.

Tint – The lighter value of a color obtained by mixing with white.

Toggle bolt – A wall anchor that forms a brace inside the wall; used on hollow walls where wood-framing studs are absent.

Topper – A window treatment that only covers the top portion of the window; a valance.

Topstitch – Machine stitching on the right (top) side of an item for decorative or functional purposes, often along the edge.

Trompe l'oeil – French for "fool the eye." A flat object is painted to appear three-dimensional.

T-square – A measuring device that is in the shape of a T; usually found in art supply or hardware stores.

Tulle – Fine, sheer, net fabric.

U

Upholsterer's tape – A strip that is used as additional reinforcing.

Uplighting – Light that is usually from a lower source that beams vertically.

V

Valance – A fabric top treatment for windows.

Value – The degree of lightness or darkness of a color. For example, lilac is a light value of purple, whereas eggplant is a dark value. Light values are called tints and dark values are called shades.

Varnish – A final transparent layer that protects the painted layers it covers.

Veneer – A thin layer of wood that is bonded to a wood surface of lesser quality.

Verdigris – A green coating that forms on copper and bronze when they are exposed to the atmosphere; it can also be created through a decorative painting technique.

Voile – A fine, sheer fabric that is crisp to the touch.

W

Wainscoting – Paneling that goes only part way up a wall and is usually topped with a chair rail.

Woodgraining – The natural lines in a piece of wood; it can also be created with a decorative painting technique and a special woodgraining tool (available in craft stores and home centers).

Wood putty – A substance that is used to fill holes in wood and furniture; it can be stained to match the surrounding area.

Index

McCall's Patterns by Donna Babylon

Donna Babylon's new home decorating pattern collection—*More Splash Than Cash*™—is part of The McCall Pattern Company's Spring 1999 collection. The initial four patterns offer creativity and versatility in each group of projects. All the fabrics featured in the collection are 54-inch-wide home decorating fabrics.

The More Splash Than Cash Spring 1999 Pattern Collection

McCall's 2065, Table Runners and Place Mats – This design features traditional and contemporary fabrics in formal and casual table runners. Donna's unique place mats echo the edging on the table runners for a finished look.

McCall's 2066, Sack Pillows – In this unique design, each pillow is covered not once, but twice! First a knife-edged pillow is covered with fabric. This covered pillow is then slipped into its own decorative sack finished with fabric ties at one side so the covered pillow peeks out.

McCall's 2164, Storage Cover-Ups – These days nearly everyone has a few utilitarian storage holders. They're the obvious solution to many storage needs, but they let in dust. The solution? Fabric cover-ups! For easy access to the contents each storage container features grommets and ties, roll-up sides, bow closures, and flaps that fold back.

McCall's 2165, Fabric Headboards – Turn your bedroom into a cozy retreat with padded fabric headboards. All four hanging headboards are mounted on decorative hardware and each is finished with beautiful sconces or finials.

Purchase McCall s
More Splash Than Cash™ Patterns

Look for **McCall's More Splash Than Cash™** patterns at your local fabric retailer or order directly from McCall's. Simply fill out the coupon below and send a check or money order (no cash or stamps, please) for the appropriate amount to the proper address.

In the United States, mail to:
The McCall Pattern Company
Splash Than Cash Offer 1999
P. O. Box 3889
Manhattan, KS 66505-8520

In Canada, mail to:
The McCall Pattern Company
Splash Than Cash Offer 1999
205 Bethridge Road
Etobicoke, Ontario
M9W 1N4 Canada

I would like to order these patterns at $11.95 each

_____ McCall's 2065 Table Runners,
        Place Mats, & Napkins
_____ McCall's 2066 Pillows
_____ McCall's 2164 Storage Cover-ups
_____ McCall's 2165 Fabric Headboards

[   ] McCall's pattern(s) at
        $11.95 each .... $_____
        (Shipping & handling included)
Residents of CA, FL, GA, IL, KS, NY and WA
add applicable sales tax. .... $_____
Total amount enclosed for
        U.S. residents .... $[_____]

Canada residents:
Please send the total above in
        Canadian funds .... $_____
Add 7% GST .... $_____
or, where applicable, add 15% HST . $_____
Ontario residents add 8% PST .... $_____
Quebec residents add 7 1/2% QST .. $_____
Total amount enclosed in
        Canadian funds .... $[_____]

(please print)
Name _____
Address _____
_____ Apt. _____
City _____ State _____ Zip _____
Country _____
Please make check or money order payable to **The McCall Pattern Company**. Please allow six to eight weeks from our receipt of order for delivery. Offer must be postmarked by February 1, 2000.

McCall s 2065

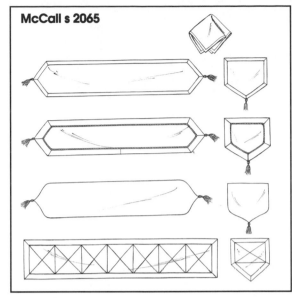

McCall s 2066

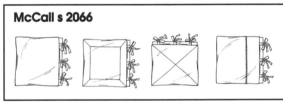

McCall s 2164

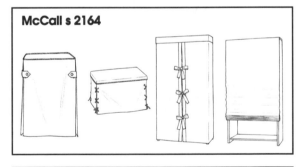

McCall s 2165

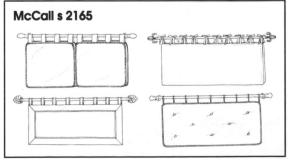

Meet
Donna Babylon

Donna Babylon is a nationally known educator, author, public speaker and television personality in the home decorating and sewing industries. Through her books and national media appearances, she has broadened her appeal beyond traditional home sewers to include millions of Americans who are interested in decorating their homes themselves.

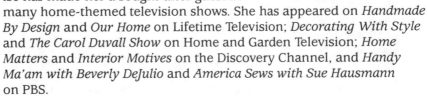

Her personable, easy-going manner, plus her ability to entertain as she educates has made her a popular speaker at national and regional sewing shows including the prestigious *Sewing and Stitchery Expo* in Puyallup, Washington, with over 30,000 do-it-yourselfers in attendance each year.

JEFFREY F. BILL

Her floor-to-ceiling, wall-to-wall expertise has made her a sought-after guest in many home-themed television shows. She has appeared on *Handmade By Design* and *Our Home* on Lifetime Television; *Decorating With Style* and *The Carol Duvall Show* on Home and Garden Television; *Home Matters* and *Interior Motives* on the Discovery Channel, and *Handy Ma'am with Beverly DeJulio* and *America Sews with Sue Hausmann* on PBS.

Donna Babylon has written twelve home decorating books covering subjects such as quilting, valances, pillows, and lampshades. Her best-selling book, *Versatile Valances*, has helped hundreds of thousands of people make beautiful window treatments for their homes. In 1997 she wrote *The Total Bedroom* (That Patchwork Place) and *How to Dress a Naked Window* (Krause Publications).

Donna lives in Baltimore, Maryland with her two cats, Ashley and Murphy. In her free time, she is an avid bicyclist and downhill skier.

Visit Donna's website, www.DonnaBabylon.com to learn about her other books, television appearances, seminar schedule, her decorating tips and more.

✪ther 𝒷ooks by 𝒟onna 𝒷abylon

Donna Babylon has authored several books on home decorating. They are available by mail from Windsor Oak Publishing or on Donna's website.

How to Dress a Naked Window. $19.95
Shipping (each book).................................. 3.50
This book will give you inspiration and practical know-how to create window treatments that are packed with personality. The book offers professional tips so you can create a custom look for a fraction of the price. Complete instructions for over 30 window treatments. Completely illustrated and full color photos.

Versatile Valances $7.95
Shipping (each book).................................. 1.75
This instructional book features tried and true methods for making 15 easy rod pocket valances. These easy projects are perfect for beginners. Completely illustrated and full color photos.

Shade Parade $8.95
Shipping (each book).................................. 1.75
Spruce up your existing lampshades with fabric, trim, flowers and a little creativity. This book offers over 20 ways to embellish lampshades. A fun project to undertake. Completely illustrated and full color photos.

Send check or money order (U.S. funds only) to:

Windsor Oak Publishing
2043 East Joppa Road, Suite 354
Baltimore, MD 21234

These books and others by Donna Babylon available on her website:

www.DonnaBabylon.com